THE
DVINA REMAINS

THE
DVINA
REMAINS

EUGENIE FRASER

MAINSTREAM
PUBLISHING

EDINBURGH AND LONDON

Key to group photograph on the jacket:

My young Uncle Yura with his bicycle, next to him my mother, next to her my Russian grandmother, sitting beside her is my Uncle Hendry on leave from India, next to him my Scots grandmother and beside her my father with my young brother. I am sitting on the grass. Behind them is a friend of the family Mr Pavlov, beside him Uncle Sanya (my father's brother), next to him Uncle Vanya, (Babushka's brother). This was taken on a hot summer's day in 1912.

First published in Great Britain in 1996 by
MAINSTREAM PUBLISHING COMPANY (EDINBURGH) LTD
7 Albany Street
Edinburgh EH1 3UG

ISBN 1 85158 839 6

Subsidised by the  THE SCOTTISH ARTS COUNCIL

Typeset in Adobe Garamond by Litho Link Ltd, Welshpool, Powys, Wales
Printed and bound in Great Britain by Butler & Tanner Ltd, Frome

CONTENTS

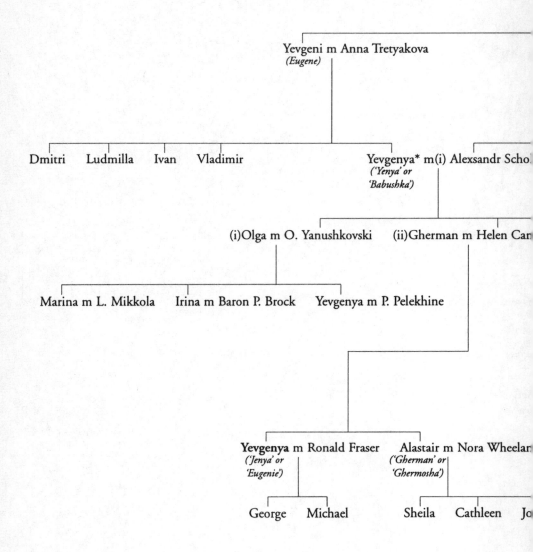

Yevgeni m Anna Tretyakova
(Eugene)

Dmitri   Ludmilla   Ivan   Vladimir   Yevgenya* m(i) Alexsandr Scho
                                                                           ('Yenya' or
                                                                            'Babushka')

(i)Olga m O. Yanushkovski   (ii)Gherman m Helen Car

Marina m L. Mikkola   Irina m Baron P. Brock   Yevgenya m P. Pelekhine

Yevgenya m Ronald Fraser   Alastair m Nora Wheelar
('Jenya' or   *('Gherman' or*
'Eugenie')   *'Ghermosha')*

George   Michael   Sheila   Cathleen   Jo

n Gernet m Margaretha Van Brienen

Amelia m Franz Scholts

Adolph m Fanny DesFontaines

Aleksandr m Shura Kisleva   Adya   Franz   Fanny   Marguniya

:vgeni m Elena Orlova   (ii)Victoria m Kyrill ?   ?(iii)Olga m Victor Aurnatov   (iv)Aleksandr m Katya
Evgenie   *('Vika')*   *('Shurick')*
'Jenya',
usin of
uthor)

Sergei   Nataliya
eryozha')   *('Natasha')*

Dr A. Popov m(ii) Yevgenya*

(i)Margarita m D. Danilov   (ii)Sergei m Masha ?   (iii)Georg m Manya ?
                                    (Uncle   *('Yura')*
                                  'Seryozha')

Liza   Vladimir   Nikolai   Yuri   Nina   Alexei

Chapter 1

RUSSIA REVISITED

IT ALL BEGAN one Sunday in June 1972 when the sky was cloudless, the sun shone warmly and the sweet scent of lilac was wafting over our flower garden where my husband Ronald and I were spending a peaceful afternoon. I was on my kneeler, clearing the weeds from the rose bed while Ronald, lying on his sun-chair (forbidden to do any weeding since the day when, trimming the edges of the lawn, he removed the heads of my precious gentians), was idly scanning some travel brochures. All was serene until quite casually he announced that this year we could spend our holidays in Russia.

'Russia!' I had echoed, leaping up from my kneeler in horrified astonishment. 'How could I go to Russia when in my passport it is clearly stated that I was born in Archangel? The K.G.B. are liable to ask questions and even arrest me if they wished to do so on any trumped-up charge.'

'Your passport,' Ronald was quick to point out, 'is British. You are a British subject with a Scot for a husband into the bargain. There's nothing to fear. Besides,' he added, 'I should very much like to see this Russia, about which I have been hearing for many a long year. The company Sov-Scot, he continued, 'is offering remarkable value – £180 for the two of us to Leningrad, Moscow and Sochi, covering all extras. It could be a wonderful holiday; so why not go?'

In the end, after further discussions, the longing to see Russia (after an absence of more than fifty years) overcame my misgivings.

Our journey commenced from Glasgow in early August. There we followed a lively throng of passengers boarding the Aeroflot flight to Leningrad, but once inside we found all double seats were occupied, forcing Ronald to take a seat next the passage and settle down with *The Scotsman* while I sat opposite beside a window. On the adjacent seat lay a coat and hat, obviously a reservation for someone still due to arrive. He duly did. A tall, well-built man, he appeared to have some connection with the Sov-Scot organisation and was acquainted with the young stewardess with whom he held a conversation in Russian prior to settling down beside me. He was Scottish – a pleasant man, with a good knowledge of the Russian language. Having introduced ourselves we talked together throughout the journey in Russian and English. He told me that he had always admired Russia and her people and late in life succeeded in learning the language.

Time passed quickly. At one stage of our journey when I was looking down on a wide expanse of water studded with islands, my companion informed me that that was Finland. Soon there was the fastening of belts, the landing on the runway, a faint shuddering, a stop – I was in Russia! As we prepared to disembark I was surprised to see my friend give Ronald a furtive tap on the shoulder with the whispered admonition – 'Leave *The Scotsman* on the seat. Do *not* take it with you!' Ronald took the hint.

It is difficult to describe my feelings as I stepped off the plane and found myself standing on Russian soil after an absence of so many long years – the strange sense of unreality from hearing the passers-by speaking in my native tongue.

On arriving in front of the immigration officer, the young man checking my passport looked up and smiled. 'And so you have returned,' he said in Russian. 'But why here? Why not Archangel?'

I smiled back. 'Yes, why not?' I answered. 'If you will allow me?' There was no response. Archangel was a closed city.

In the reception hall a lot of people were milling around and standing in their midst was my fellow traveller. I caught his eye, but as I moved towards him to say a few words he turned his back to me. After our *bonhomie* on the plane such rudeness was astonishing, but later Ronald was to endure a similar experience when we all met up again in Moscow. It then became obvious we were not considered desirable acquaintances and, not being 'one of them', were to be avoided.

Eventually our group was shown to a room upstairs where we gathered around a long table for our first meal in Russia – a meal which could have been described as a dire warning of what to expect during our stay. A great deal of building work was going on around us with workers and waitresses passing to and fro while nearby a long queue of people – some of whom seemed desperate – had formed at the door of what appeared to be the only toilet available.

A tour had been organised to take us around Leningrad, prior to boarding the night train for Moscow, but by the time we joined the bus dusk had fallen and it was not possible to enjoy a clear view of the city. The young and pleasant girl who was our guide brightened up the picture by pointing out the various places of interest and telling us all about them as we toured around the city.

By hearing such names as 'Nevsky Prospect', I was reminded of my former sojourn in St Petersburg (as Leningrad was then known and as it is again now) with my family in 1912, when my father was there on business. A distant scene came back quite clearly of a lovely summer day when I, with Ghermosha, my young brother, set off with our parents for a walk on Nevsky Prospect. We had halted beside an old man selling balloons and my father bought one for both of us, but a few minutes later the string slipped through my fingers. As I stood watching in despair my lovely balloon rose high into the clouds and vanished out of sight. Soon the same disaster occurred to my young brother, but in his case the balloon did not float upwards but sailed across the road. Before anyone could stop me, and ignoring the traffic, I rushed in hot pursuit in a vain attempt to catch it – only to be knocked down by a passing youth on a bicycle.

Luckily no one was hurt and the bicycle was undamaged. After giving me a good scolding – and the young boy a little backhander – our walk continued. There were to be no more balloons.

Later in the year we were again strolling along the elegant Nevsky Prospect, but then it was winter with snow, sparkling frosted pavements and cold sunshine. St Petersburg was preparing for Christmas and wore a festive air. The shops were spilling over with their bright and varied merchandise. We sauntered slowly, soon to be attracted by crowds of people standing beside the window of a confectioner renowned for his chocolates. Against a background of black and crimson was a strange design of chocolate boxes fashioned in the shape of mice – pale grey with crimson collars and trembling tails. I longed to possess such a box and begged my parents to buy one but all my pleas were ignored. The following evening while curled up on the top bunk in a compartment of a train thundering to Archangel – the box was on my lap!

I had been sent ahead of my parents to my Russian babushka (granny) under the care of a friend – a young man who had been studying music at the Conservatoire in St Petersburg and was now returning to Archangel. My father, to soften the sadness of my departure, had presented to me a parcel with the instructions that I was to open it after the train left the station. On opening the box I found inside small chocolate mice wrapped in silver foil complete with crimson collars, beady eyes and trembling tails. I was six years old and played for hours with these fascinating creatures – never eating a single one. They helped to break the monotony of a journey lasting two days and nights, but with the excitement of arriving in Archangel and meeting my beloved babushka, the box was left behind.

Four years later in 1916 I was back in St Petersburg – by then renamed Petrograd. My brother, Ghermosha, and I, together with our mother, had been staying with friends at their small estate which was situated near a village known as 'Dobroye Syelo' – 'Kind Village' – and were now spending a few days in their town flat, prior to returning to Archangel.

Petrograd had the sad appearance of a city at war. The war, now approaching its third year, was going badly for Russia. Young as I was, I sensed a certain anxiety in the air, an anxiety likewise expressed by our friends who talked about going abroad. Mingling with the jostling crowd on the Nevsky

Prospect were uniformed men representing the various forces, some of whom were obvious casualties.

One evening Mother decided to take Ghermosha and me to a popular cinema known as 'Parisyana'. In the foyer was a life-size portrait of a famous film star of the time who bore the strange name of Vera Holodnaya – 'Vera Cold'. Below the enormous black picture hat was a beautiful face with large soulful eyes. Under this glamorous portrait some wit had written in large letters 'She needs to be warmed up', which Ghermosha and I thought was extremely funny! The film could not have made any impression on me as I have no memory of it whatsoever.

The following day we set off for a stroll along the Nevsky Prospect, where we halted to admire a flower shop. Wheedling some money out of my mother, I bought a large pot of beautiful blue hydrangeas for my babushka. We left that same night for Archangel. For two days and nights I cradled and fussed over that precious package and on arrival proudly presented it to my babushka to her great delight. Little did we know that a mere six months later there would be a revolution followed by a take-over by Lenin's Bolsheviks. This led to the gradual destruction of our way of life culminating in 1920 in the abandonment, at his insistence, of our father (by then blind and crippled in his sick bed) and, together with Mother, our final sad departure from Archangel – eventually arriving, after a horrendous flight by sea to Norway, on the doorsteps of our Scots grandparents' house in Broughty Ferry. Now here I was sitting in a bus travelling through the streets of Leningrad on the way to the station to board a train for Moscow.

The sleeping compartment allotted to us was shared by two young women – a situation which in Britain might have been described as unusual but not so in Russia. With a little skilful manipulation we succeeded in avoiding any embarrassing incidents. Ronald obligingly went out into the corridor while the girls and I undressed and hopped into our bunks. He then discreetly undressed and settled in the bunk below me. The girls were a cheerful pair who were with another group of tourists going on to Kiev after Moscow. Our compartment was quite spacious and comfortably provided with clean linen and covers.

We awoke early and having dressed, stood in the corridor watching the passing scenery. I had expected to see lush meadows and attractive villages but instead there appeared to be a succession of factories, a few birches here and there and on the whole, a rather monotonous landscape.

In due course we arrived in Moscow where we boarded a bus which took us to the Hotel Bucharest. A friendly young woman directed us into a spacious bedroom with an adjoining, well-furnished sitting-room. There was also a small toilet with WC, washbasin and ample hot water. In the washbasin, however, we found no plug, but having been warned previously, we had brought our own.

To have a shower it was necessary to go down to the basement where everything was in order and likewise clean.

From our window looking across the Moscow river, we had the enchanting view of St Basil's Cathedral with its soaring, bulbous domes, each unique in colour and design – a scene straight out of some ancient Russian fairy tale. To the right on the opposite side of the river could be seen the gigantic Hotel Russia – reputed to be the largest hotel in Russia.

In contrast to the comfort of our room were the chaotic conditions reigning in the dining-room. Due to numerous conferences taking place in Moscow our hotel was overcrowded, with the inexperienced staff unable to deal with such an influx of people from various parts of Russia as well as the foreign tourists. In addition Moscow was suffering from an unprecedented heat-wave – a tropical heat, we were told and unknown in living memory.

The meals for our group throughout our stay were served upstairs above the main overcrowded dining-room. On our arrival, Ronald and I were directed to a table where we were joined by two other couples with whom we soon formed our own little group for the duration of our stay in Russia. Time has erased the names of one couple, but we still remember Jean and John Begg whose humour and wit enlivened our stay.

A young and rather harassed girl brought some boiled eggs, bread and butter and a very small teapot with only sufficient tea for three cups. I approached our guide, Nona, who was hovering around and eventually a second large teapot was dumped on the table. This one unfortunately contained only hot water. We saw the funny side of that and gave up the unequal struggle. The service, however, improved a bit as time went on.

What I did discover was that the most welcome tourist was one who was either a dedicated communist or one who did not know a word of Russian. Tourists are necessary and those who had left Russia during the revolution had to be tolerated but at the same time watched and not drawn into any warm conversation.

Nona was an attractive young woman who spoke perfect English and was gushingly welcoming to many of the tourists but when I approached her and spoke in Russian, her answers were short and accompanied by a cold, hard stare.

I then had the strange experience, after a tour round the Kremlin, when Tanya, our other guide who had replaced Nona, spoke to me in a friendly manner in one of the cathedrals and during our conversation remarked that the old Russians were always recognised by the purity of their spoken Russian. This surprised me as after so many years there were many words I had forgotten. Later, while sitting in the bus awaiting the others, I repeated this conversation to my husband in English. There were a few people in the bus as well as the driver who glanced across at me. The following morning Nona appeared on the scene and announced that Tanya had taken ill, and that she was resuming control. This incident worried me a bit. I kept asking myself if I was responsible for Tanya's sudden removal.

One day, perhaps moved by a morbid curiosity, I suggested to Ronald that we should join the lengthy queue waiting to enter Lenin's mausoleum. Inside, in the chilly twilight, the curious onlookers moved silently in single file past the recumbent figure under his glass cover. I saw nothing in these mediocre features except that this was the face of a being responsible for the destruction of the way of life of a great nation and the suffering and death of countless millions of innocent people including friends and members of my own family. It was a relief to escape from that gloomy morgue into the bright sunshine.

The whole concept of the mausoleum, with the mummified corpse and the strutting guards, was nothing more than an absurd exhibition of bad taste and in fairness to Lenin would never have met with his approval. He wished only to be buried beside his mother.

During the five days spent in Moscow there were the usual guided tours around the city, some of absorbing interest such as the Kremlin with the ancient, magnificent cathedrals, and others rather tedious and long since forgotten. We preferred to set off on our own and surprisingly no one ever stopped us.

We planned one day to visit the Novodevichi nunnery, a place of great historical interest and where at one time Peter the Great had his sister, Tsarevna Sophia, incarcerated. The nunnery, however, was closed that day. We strolled instead around the adjoining cemetery, the resting place of many famous people. The grave of Lenin's brother, executed for attempting to blow up Alexander the Third, aroused a passing interest. There was also the poignant and beautifully sculpted statue of Stalin's wife, Nadezhda Allilueva, who shot herself in helpless despair after she had learned of the suffering and butchering of so many innocent people. As I stood studying this tragic figure a question flashed through my mind – why was it that she had not shot her monstrous husband instead? Millions of lives might have been spared if she had.

Back in the Red Square we joined a small queue of tourists waiting to enter St Basil's Church. To our surprise the interior of St Basil's was in complete contrast to the enchanting exterior. We moved in gloomy darkness through a succession of small rooms, where the ancient walls seemed to exude a strange, uncanny sensation as if we were transported back over the long centuries to the cruel reign of Ivan the Terrible. We kept hurrying, stumbling over the uneven flooring, the high steps and almost ran down the stairway out into the open square, much relieved to join the milling throng of pedestrians.

When we were there, St Basil's was being restored but I heard recently that church services are being held inside – something I find difficult to imagine.

Better by far was the trip on one of the steamers that ply up and down the Moskva river. It was good to relax, to feel a cool breeze caressing one's face, to watch the passing scenery, the golden domes of the Kremlin, a glimpse of a beautiful church at the far end of a side street, people strolling in a leafy park or lying on grassy banks. In the air was a pervading smell of smoke and half burned logs were floating down the river.

During our stay large fires were raging in the woods outside Moscow and all over town posters warned the public of the danger of more fires breaking out due to the abnormally high temperature. A little boy, wearing a large cowboy hat, which appeared to give him much pleasure, kept coming over to chat to us. He was a friendly child but his parents, beyond uncertain smiles, did not break into any conversation.

After reaching the final landing stage we sailed back on the same steamer, but arrived later than we had expected and by the time we joined our friends in the dining-room of the 'Bucharest' they were finishing the second course.

Our usual waitress came over and in resentful tones admonished me. 'You are late, madam!' She was young – a poor, wearied, little soul, quite exhausted, but like a defiant child she repeated, 'You are late, madam!'

'Yes, my dear,' I agreed and touched her hand. 'It does not matter, we are not hungry. Just serve us the third course.'

The little face crumpled, tears welled up in her eyes. 'I am so tired, madam, and my poor feet are so sore. I have been on them since six o'clock this morning. I wish I had never left my village.' She went away but soon returned and, smiling through her tears, served us with the third course. It was not surprising that the girl was so upset. Too many of these young waitresses appeared to have little or no experience and were probably engaged on a temporary basis.

By now, between the heat, the overcrowded dining-room and what must have been far from desirable conditions in the kitchen, too many people in our group were beginning to suffer from stomach upsets, including Ronald and some of our friends. Only those who brought with them remedial medicines or were blessed with a strong immunity escaped these unpleasant symptoms which actually continued, even in Sochi where conditions were very good. I was fortunate in having an inbuilt resistance, probably due to having survived a period of near starvation in my youth in Archangel during the aftermath of the revolution when we ate anything and everything we could find. In this way I must have developed a certain immunity which was to stand me in good stead later when in India, where upset stomachs were by no means a rarity. In spite of these unpleasant attacks, everybody continued going out, seeing places and making the most of the few days left in Moscow.

One afternoon, deciding to purchase some postcards to send to our friends, we set off for the renowned 'Dom Knig' – 'The House of Books' – in the Arbat district. As the stance was on the opposite side of the river, we crossed the bridge and duly boarded the bus where, to our dismay, we had to produce the exact fare. Not having any small change, we realised we would have to get off, but at this stage an elderly woman got up from her seat and paid our fare. I thanked her gratefully and offered the money that we had, but she only smiled and shook her head.

As we continued travelling, the bus became overcrowded with some people standing. Afraid that we might be taken beyond our station I approached a pleasant looking man, standing beside the entrance, and asked him where we should get off. 'You have a bit to go yet. I'll tell you when you have to leave,' he said and then continued in a friendly way asking me the usual questions as to where we came from and how did we like Moscow. It was all very congenial until I said, 'You must also come to visit us in Scotland.'

His demeanour changed abruptly. 'We don't need to leave our country to see any places abroad.' He went on, his face darkening as he spoke. 'Russia has everything. No one could show us anything better.'

His sudden, uncalled for rudeness offended me. 'Yes,' I rejoined coldly, 'that might be so, but Scotland also has a lot to offer. It is known to be a beautiful country.'

'Every duck thinks her own pond is best,' he answered, and lapsed into a morose silence.

We were now approaching our stop. 'This is where you get off,' he said in a more congenial manner. I nodded coldly but did not answer. Later I understood the reason for his defensive attitude. Very few Russians are allowed to travel abroad. An invitation such as mine only served as a reminder that he was a prisoner in his own country.

Inside the 'House of Books', after our enquiry regarding postcards, we were directed to the floor above, where we were assured we would find a good selection. There I approached a young girl standing behind the counter with her cheek resting on the palm of her hand. She appeared to be deep in thought. 'Can you tell me, please,' I enquired 'where we can find some postcards?'

She didn't even turn her pretty head, '*Ya ne znayou,*' ('I don't know') she said, obviously resenting my intrusion. A few paces round the corner of her counter, however, we found our postcards and bought a few.

Beyond the purchasing of the postcards and the incident with the indolent sales girl I cannot recall anything of our visit to the 'Dom Knig'.

Later, while strolling along the Kalinin's Prospect, we were attracted by a rich display of cakes, cookies and bread in the window of a patisserie. Tempted by some appetising looking rolls, I went inside and joined the queue of people waiting to be served. When my turn came the sales girl handed me a slip but not my purchase! With this slip I had to go over to the cash desk where a second queue had formed and where, after standing for some time, I paid for my purchase and returned with the receipt to join once more by now the third queue, at the end of which on handing over the receipt I received my rolls!

I was astonished and cannot recollect ever seeing such an insane procedure anywhere else. How frustrating such a system must be to a hard-working mother hurrying home to prepare a meal for her family.

Continuing on our way, we eventually found ourselves in Arbat Street where we halted to admire a display of paintings in an art shop and went inside. The shop was empty except for an elderly man who was standing beside the counter with great reverence inspecting a large portrait of Lenin which, with the same ardent reverence, was duly carefully packed and carried away by the delighted purchaser.

Meanwhile we were browsing around, halting here and there to study a picture. Not being experts, we occasionally buy something which pleases us, irrespective of whom the artist may be.

Nothing appealed to me until, just as we were leaving, I caught sight of a picture in a cheap frame hanging on the wall. It depicted a wintry garden, tall stark trees in deep snow, the faint line of a river behind them, the crimson glow of the setting sun. To the left was a large house with twinkling lights in the windows.

I stood studying the scene. I remembered a long-lost world and myself as a young girl, eight years old, all alone in the sleeping garden, skiing between the trees, over the sparkling snowdrifts encircling an empty summer house with the dark pines like sentinels guarding the approach, until, afraid of the encroaching shadows and strange silence, I would skim over the snow-covered gates and hurry back to the warmth of the house, the purring samovar, the welcoming smiles.

We bought the picture by an anonymous artist and carried it back to Scotland. We planned a handsome frame for it, but it still hangs as it was, a gentle reminder of my distant childhood.

During the last few days of our stay in Moscow we attended a performance in a theatre situated within walking distance on our side of the river, just beyond the British Embassy.

It was a memorable evening. To my amazement I heard again the traditional songs of the troika drivers sung in the old Russian style by an elderly artist with a magnificent voice and enjoyed a brilliant performance by a balalaika orchestra.

In looking back, however, to these torrid days in Moscow what stands out in my memory is what became the highlight of our whole trip. It so happened that on that same evening there had been organised a talk on 'Friendship' for the benefit of the tourists. Having not the slightest desire to listen to a lot of nonsense in the form of Soviet propaganda we decided to branch out on our own, have dinner in some restaurant and hopefully meet a Russian or two with whom we could converse and spend a congenial evening.

We approached the lady at the reception desk. Willing to answer all enquiries, she tried to help us but unfortunately when phoning to the various restaurants to arrange a booking the answer was a simple *No* – all the tables were fully booked. It was the pleasant doorman who came to our rescue. 'Try The Slavanski Bazaar,' he suggested. 'It is usually possible to find a place there if you are prepared to wait for it.'

'The Slavanski Bazaar' was the name of a hotel renowned for being mentioned by Chekhov in his stories, a place where he stayed on several occasions as did his friend, the famous singer Chaliapin.

Following the instructions of the doorman and because Ron also remembered having seen the place one day, we found it with comparative ease – now, it would seem, no longer a hotel but a very flourishing restaurant. Inside, we joined the queue in the corridor adjoining the restaurant from where we could hear the band playing and the steady hum of voices. Periodically, a plump lady dressed in black and heavily made-up, appeared on the scene to lead someone inside.

Standing in front of us was a young couple too engrossed in each other to be interested in any foreigners. In due course the lady in black appeared and directed the pair to a vacant table – but no sooner did they vanish inside than they came out again. Turning to us the girl said, 'You can go now – we shall wait.' Such behaviour was puzzling until when passing them I overheard the girl say to her escort, 'How could we possibly have shared a table with such uncultured people!'

We were shown to a table for six. Seated at the far top was a young blonde with an uptilted little nose and dressed in pink – quite attractively. She glanced coldly in our direction and turned away to speak to her partner, a handsome Georgian sitting at the corner, beside whom I was placed. Opposite us were two young men, obviously workmen, out to enjoy themselves. Each, having dispensed with fork and knife, was nibbling away happily at half a chicken, washed down with iced coffee and vodka – time about. We realised that this was the lack of culture that had driven the young couple away!

The Muscovites were enjoying themselves. At the top of the hall a band was playing with great style and vigour, while standing beside them, an attractive brunette was singing in full voice as only Russians can sing. On the dance floor couples were circling around – some in tight embrace, oblivious of the exhausting heat – a heat greater than anything I had ever experienced in India, and that without the punkahs or air-conditioning that might have made it bearable.

A waitress, looking hot and bothered, came over with the menu. The list of dishes was long and varied but only some were available. Ice-cream, in which the Russians usually excel, had melted away. The fridge had broken down and the milk was sour. Yet before me is the little slip, kept over these long years, which tells me we did not do too badly. We had been served a variety of fish, meat cutlets, salads, vegetables, pancakes with a sweet sauce, black coffee, the ever popular *kvass* (a light beer made from rye bread and yeast) and, of course, a carafe of vodka. The total cost for all these items was ten roubles and a few kopecks which, according to the rate of exchange prevailing at that time, was equivalent to a mere five pounds sterling!

As is usual in Russia, a considerable time elapsed before our order appeared on the table though it has to be said that the food was good and far superior to what was served in the 'Bucharest'. Meanwhile, my Georgian neighbour on hearing me conversing with Ronald enquired if we came from England. 'No,' I rejoined, 'we are from Scotland.'

'What does your husband do?' he asked.

'My husband,' I explained, 'was general manager over a group of jute mills in India in Calcutta but has now retired to Scotland, the land of his birth.'

'Calcutta,' the Georgian said, 'is famous for beautiful carpets.'

'No,' I corrected him gently, 'it's Mirzapur that is famous for carpets. In Calcutta the main industry is jute.'

My friend was obviously nettled at being told he was mistaken. 'I can assure you,' he insisted, 'woollen carpets are manufactured in Calcutta. I have been there several times and know what I am talking about.'

At this point one of the young men who had been listening with great interest, turned to Ronald. 'Do they make carpets in Calcutta?' he enquired. Ronald understood enough Russian simply to say the one word '*nikogda*' meaning 'never'. A smile of satisfaction lit up the faces of the two lads who had been treated with silent contempt by the proud Georgian and his escort.

No Georgian likes to be contradicted by a female and at this stage it was the girlfriend who stepped into the breach by suggesting it was time to leave. My Georgian friend stood up and bowed politely and his partner, who up to now had not uttered a single word to us, when passing the table, nodded proudly and said in a rather affected, drawn-out manner, 'Goodbye,' perhaps to show that she likewise knew the English language.

With only four people now remaining at the table the atmosphere became relaxed. The boys glancing uncertainly at us were as yet too shy to break into conversation. One of them, whose name I learned later was Misha, kept fanning himself with a folded newspaper. His friend, to whom I shall refer as Volodya, seeing me constantly dabbing my face with a handkerchief, turned to Misha. 'Can't you see how hot she is? Give her your newspaper.' Misha duly obliged but I, instead of fanning myself, spread it in front of me and began to read the headings. This proved too much for Misha. 'Excuse me, please,' he said, 'we have heard you speaking in Russian, but did not think that you could read it as well. Where did you learn our language?'

'In Arhangelsk,' I laughed, 'where I was born and brought up.' From that moment all inhibitions were cast aside. A string of questions followed. 'Where did we live? – Did we own our house? Do all the ladies in Scotland wear these mini-skirts?' I answered as best as I could. 'We live in Scotland. Yes, we do own our house. Only young ladies wear mini-skirts, elderly ladies never do.'

'They put us off our work,' was the laughing rejoinder. More questions followed. 'Is it true that all married women sit at home, taking care of the house while the men go out to work?'

'At one time that was so,' I explained, 'but nowadays many women work as well as their husbands.'

'Do you work?' Volodya asked.

'At sixty-six,' I told him, 'I would be considered too old to work.'

'Our women have to work very hard,' he commented sadly, 'and look much older than you do.'

They were young, intelligent and immensely interested in all we had to say. 'To us you are from another world,' Misha remarked and to my surprise added, 'You do not mind talking to us – after all, we are only bricklayers.' This saddened me. No man that I knew of in Scotland would have demeaned himself by asking such a question.

'We are,' we hastened to tell them, 'very happy to be with you. It is the best evening we have spent in Moscow – never to be forgotten,' which indeed it was and is still remembered. Later, as the hours went by and the tables emptied, we all stood up and drank to friendship.

'To *druzhba*' (friendship), they repeated, as we embraced in the old Russian style.

Outside the night was peaceful, the air pleasantly cool after the heat of the restaurant. High above in the sapphire sky, the moon was shedding her magical radiance. Crossing the Red Square, we were rewarded by the rare and wonderful sight of the Kremlin, the great assemblage of towers, spires, cathedrals and golden cupolas all bathed in this heavenly light – a scene of enchanting splendour.

Although it was late, we decided prior to returning to the 'Bucharest' to inspect some of the Metro Stations where we hoped to find the famous sculptures. On going down to the nearest station we approached the floor lady at the bottom of the escalator to ask for information.

In this particular metro there were a few sculptures, but apart from a vague memory of a peasant girl standing with a sheaf of corn in her arms, and a man

20

with a dog, I have no recollection of any other sculptures. What stands out in these palatial stations of mosaics and marble is the immaculate order and cleanliness. Here there is no graffiti, no dirt, no danger from hooligans, but an orderly throng of people moving up and down the escalator.

While we were talking to the sociable floor lady, a middle-aged man approached us. Well dressed, with a pleasant manner, he enquired if he could help us. On hearing about our interest in sculptures he informed us that the best sculptures were in another metro station and if we wished he would be pleased to escort us there and show us around. We, however, realising that it was later than we had imagined and remembering that on the following day we were due to fly to Sochi, decided not to go to the other station but to take the first train which would take us to the station close to the 'Bucharest'. It transpired that our kindly stranger lived in the same district and so the three of us travelled together.

He was a friendly soul and had obviously been out with the boys as there was a faint aroma of vodka wafting over us. His name and line of business is long since forgotten. He had been through the war and fought in the battle for Stalingrad – as it was known at that time. 'There was no mercy there,' he had added, drawing his hand across his throat, 'no quarter given by either side.' He had been badly wounded but somehow survived and was now living with his wife and son in a two-roomed flat. 'Nothing much to look forward to,' he concluded.

On our arrival and coming out of the Metro, for some strange reason we walked in the middle of the road – perhaps, I suspect, to avoid being overheard by the passers-by on the pavements. He took my arm and held me close – to Ronald's amusement. By now the moon had vanished, leaving us walking in darkness. Our conversation continued with the usual questions and answers. 'You speak good Russian – where did you learn our language? Where do you live now and what does your husband do? When did you leave Russia?'

'In 1920 with my Scots mother and brother,' I told him.

'In 1920,' he repeated slowly, 'that was the year when all was finished, when old Russia died, the year when I was born.'

We were approaching the hotel when he stopped suddenly. 'Tell me,' he said, 'what do you think of us?'

I hesitated for a moment. 'Some are good, some bad,' I answered uncertainly.

'Yes,' he agreed, 'it's the same the whole world over but our government are *svoloch* (scum). *Proshchaite* (Goodbye). Kissing my hand and with a friendly nod to Ronald he vanished into the night.

The next day we boarded an ancient aeroplane, aptly described by our friend Jean as 'hand knitted' and thankfully landed in Sochi after an uneventful flight. 'Sochi!' – the very name takes me back to the summer of 1914 when I was promised a holiday there. I was to travel with my school friend Vanda and her parents. We both looked forward to this exciting trip, talked a lot and laid some wonderful plans – but nothing came out of them. Due to the nervous tension in the air all arrangements were cancelled. Instead, there was a holiday with my own relations in a small village near Archangel where we learned about the start of the war against Germany and hurried back to our house. Now, after all these decades, here was beautiful Sochi. Strange is fate!

We were put up in a pleasant hotel, the name of which I cannot recall. Our room, although not so spacious as the one in Moscow, was comfortable with a balcony attached. The adjoining bathroom, although supplied with the usual conveniences, we found to be very small and the washbasin with the mirror above was placed so low that Ronald when shaving had to go down on his bended knees in the open doorway before he could see himself. He was convinced that the entire bathroom must have been designed for a Georgian dwarf, but that, however, did not explain why the whole place was flooded each time we had a shower and had to wade about, ankle deep in water! Apart from these little inconveniences, we settled down happily. All meals were provided in a nearby hotel called 'Magnolia' where the food was very good and where some members of our group were fortunate to be accommodated.

We enjoyed our stay in Sochi. I, having lived in the two extremes, the arctic frosts of Russia and the exhausting heat of India, found it very pleasant to stroll about in a Mediterranean atmosphere – something quite unusual for me.

A small bus was laid on for the tourists which took us to several places of interest outside Sochi such as the beautiful garden where there grew a magnolia tree planted by Yuri Gagarin, the famous young cosmonaut who later died so tragically in a 'plane crash. The lower part of the tree was bereft of leaves – all removed to be kept as a remembrance of the tragic hero. On another day we arrived at a place where facing a square there was a huge restaurant packed with people of all ages. It transpired they were celebrating a wedding, all enjoying themselves to the accompaniment of music, vodka and zakuski.

Steps led to an open roof above, from where we were able to admire the great vista of the mountain range disappearing into the misty distance. From there also I spotted in the square below an old man selling grapes. Eager to buy some I had hurried down the steps, but when I reached his stall the grapes had vanished. 'We have no grapes for the likes of you,' he told me with an angry glint in his close-set eyes, 'we barely have enough for ourselves.'

Best of all were the shores of the Black Sea where we spent most of the mornings. As a child brought up near the White Sea on the shores of which we sometimes spent holidays and where the sea was often very stormy, with great white horses galloping across the churning waters, I somehow imagined the

Black Sea with a blue-black smooth velvet surface, peaceful and inviting. It was disappointing to find it could be just as stormy and menacing as any other.

With our bathing suits and sandals to protect our feet as the beach was not sandy but stony, we would set off for our swimming session. A pleasant walk from the hotel led us to steps going down to a concrete promenade, close to the sea. It was here that strict divisions took place between the native-born Russians and all others which included Poles, Romanians, Bulgarians, etc. Each morning we used to pass all the Russians reclining on the beach who would smile or wave a hand to us in a friendly gesture. Further along from them was a wire fence and a gate where sat an elderly woman who, after scanning our passes – still in my possession – would allow us through to join all the other foreigners. To the left were changing-rooms from which we would emerge, changed and carrying boards to let us sit on the rough stones.

On that first morning we found the sea was stormy with large waves beating against the shores. Although fond of swimming, I discovered it was quite impossible to attempt it and confined myself to wading close to the shore. Ronald, however, determined to have his swim, went out to the end of the break-water and dived in, but later when he tried to return to our beach, found it was impossible to do so and allowed himself to drift into 'enemy territory' where, after a struggle and cheered on by the watching Russians, he reached the shore. There he was immediately surrounded by a welcoming crowd who laughed and clapped his shoulders and kept repeating 'Well done dedushka' (grandpa). Later a notice was pinned up advising people not to go swimming that day.

Another day, arrangements were made to take us for a sail on the sea. We all looked forward to it but for some reason the trip was delayed and by the time we boarded the motor launch night had set in. We sailed in pitch darkness and saw nothing whatsoever. I wondered if it wasn't deliberate in case we saw something we weren't meant to see.

On the whole the people were friendly with the exception of a few whose attitude I found was rather strange.

Next to our bedroom were two men whom we took to be Georgians who were often seen standing on the balcony conversing together. One morning I came out on to the adjoining balcony and saw one of them leaning on the railings admiring the view. I smiled and wished him a good morning in Russian. The result was astonishing – one might have thought that he had been threatened by a deadly viper the way he leapt back into his room. We never saw them again.

On another morning, while Jean and I were sitting in the lower verandah enjoying a cup of coffee, we noticed a young man strolling up and down in front of us occasionally casting a glance in our direction. He eventually came over and asked if he could be permitted to join us. As we did not raise any objections, he did so and after introducing himself enquired if he might be allowed to order a bottle of champagne. With our permission, graciously granted, soon the champagne and glasses appeared on the table. At this point Ronald, who had been out for a walk, joined us. The young man – a handsome Georgian with a pleasing manner – explained that he was a dentist, but had to work very hard, at times well into the night, to augment his miserly salary so as to be able to buy little gifts for his loved one. For himself, he continued, he wished nothing, but did enjoy cigarettes – especially American brands – but the local ones were horrible. He then tentatively enquired if we could possibly buy for him from the 'Beryozka' shop attached to the hotel, a few cartons of the American Lucky Strike cigarettes. He was obviously acquainted with the 'Beryozka' shops, which offered a great variety of goods, but only for foreign currency. He had no such thing, our friend sadly explained, but would gladly pay double their value in roubles if we could provide him with perhaps eight or ten cartons. We immediately realised that before us was a pleasant but artful speculator with whom none of us had the slightest intention of getting mixed up in any deals – yet there we were partaking of his champagne and feeling slightly embarrassed. At this stage Ronald said that while he could not possibly supply such a large quantity he would buy a couple of cartons for him but accept only the current rate of exchange. It was arranged that after dinner we would meet him outside the hotel and hand over the two cartons of Lucky Strike. Our friend appeared to be quite pleased to accept this offer and took off as we went for our lunch. In the evening after dinner, true to our promise, we went for a stroll carrying the two cartons. I doubted if he would turn up, but sure enough he appeared out of nowhere, accepted his cigarettes, squared up with Ronald as arranged and vanished into the gathering dusk.

Our holiday continued with some form of diversion each day including an attendance at a circus, the best entertainment of our stay. Each act was a performance *par excellence*, whether the breath-catching flights on the trapeze, the hilarious riding of little dogs on motor-bikes and side-cars accompanied by their barking in wild excitement, obviously enjoying the fun, or the fearless Cossacks charging flat out into the ring and performing some daring feats while riding bareback.

The act of the lion tamer was particularly awesome. I have often been told that no wild animal trainer should ever turn his back on these unpredictable creatures during a performance, but there he was waltzing around with his partner while the lions sitting on their pedestals watched every moment with their strange inscrutable eyes.

On the last Sunday of our stay in Sochi I suggested to Ronald that perhaps we could find a Russian church as I would like to attend a service. I had not been to one since my departure from Russia all those long years ago.

I approached the young woman at the enquiry desk in the hotel and asked her if she could direct us to a church in the vicinity. The answer for my pains was negative. She knew of no such thing and did not think there was one in the town. For one who was a native of Sochi this was a strange answer. We decided to do some exploration on our own. After a few minutes walking through pleasant tree-lined streets, we suddenly discovered a beautiful white church, named, as we learned later, the Cathedral of St Michael. It so happened this was the sacred day of the Assumption, an event of great importance in the Orthodox faith. The church was packed with worshippers of all ages. Outside in the courtyard people were standing and in their midst were a few mental cases, described in Russia as those 'touched by the hand of God' and to be treated with great kindness.

We approached the entrance but Ronald, being in shorts, was not allowed to enter. He hurried back to the hotel to change into long trousers but by the time he returned I was inside where, from a stall selling various sacred articles, I bought a candle and a small gilt cross. From there, pushing my way into the heart of the church I found myself standing beside an old woman who, immediately recognising me as a stranger, enquired in a whisper, 'Where have you come from?' I told her I was from Scotland, but had left Archangel fifty years earlier and had never since been inside a Russian church.

'Fifty years!' she explained crossing herself in quick succession. '*Boje moi!* *Boje moi!*' (My God! My God!). A woman standing behind me touched my shoulder. 'For St Michael,' she said as she handed me a candle. 'Pass it on to the man in front of you,' the old lady instructed me. As any movement through the crowd was impossible candles were being passed over to the worshippers in front where they were lit and placed with great reverence before the various icons.

Above in the gallery christenings were taking place accompanied by the shrill protesting cries of the infants undergoing the complete immersion, thrice repeated according to the rites of the Russian Church.

It was hot to the point of discomfort, the air overlaid with the smell of incense but no one minded. All stood listening with rapt attention to the living words of the service and the magnificent singing of the choir.

The most impressive and deeply touching scene came at the end of the service when a great procession of men, women and children began to move slowly forward to receive communion, the blessing of the priest and to kiss the cross.

What also stood out is the amazing fervour and courage in the face of the greatest anti-religious campaign of this century, accompanied by the destruction of churches, monasteries and the vicious persecution of the priesthood. I was astonished and humbled by such courageous defiance.

Over all these was this strange sensation of unreality – almost uncanny as if I was transported to the long lost world of my childhood of lighted candles, familiar faces, the ancient white church, long since destroyed, that once stood on the banks of the Dvina.

To Ronald, standing at the back of the church, this was a new experience. He enjoyed the service and especially the moving unaccompanied singing of the choir.

On our return to the hotel we met some members of our group and two young Americans who, after hearing about our visit to the church, set off to attend the second service and on returning waxed eloquent about their own experience.

Two days later we said '*Proschchaite*' (Goodbye) to the sunny shores of Sochi and were off on another flight, this time to St Petersburg, renamed Leningrad, where we duly arrived and were taken to the hotel 'Russia', situated on the outskirts of the city.

From what I can recall of the hotel, our room was comfortable, the meals and service good and there was none of the hustle we experienced in Moscow. A nearby metro station provided us with quick access to the town centre any time we wished to go out on our own when it was possible to get away from the fixed schedule of sightseeing.

In St Petersburg lived two of my remaining cousins, Victoria and Evgenie, the children of my late Uncle Aleksandr, my father's brother – with whom my father lived until his death, after the departure of my mother, brother and self for Scotland in the tragic year of 1920.

I had discovered Victoria's address through her younger sister Olga who lived in New York and with whom I kept up a steady correspondence after she got in touch with me and explained why she was now living in America.

Olga had reached America after a harrowing experience when, during the last war as a young girl, she was taken prisoner by the Germans and removed to a slave labour camp in Germany, only to be rearrested by the advancing Red Army. After a miraculous escape she finally entered the free world of America whence she was later to inform me proudly – 'I am now an American citizen'.

Olga did not know the whereabouts of her brother Evgenie, but it was him, better known as Jenya, who I longed to meet. He was the eldest in the family and although much younger than me, played a large part in my childhood, almost like a small brother.

I am reminded as I write these lines how once on a bright winter's day I was sent to fetch my little cousin. A picture springs to mind of a flaxen-haired child dressed in a grey squirrel fur coat with hat to match, who is sitting on his sledge and smiling happily at me, while I, delighting in the play, am pretending I'm his pony. I remember the joyful galloping along the snowy road, between the sparkling snowdrifts, to the excited cries of '*Bistro*! *Bistro*!' (Quicker! Quicker!) from little Jenchick (as Jenya was known as a little child).

Hoping to have a happy meeting with my relatives, I wrote to Victoria giving her an approximate date for our arrival in Leningrad.

Only three days remained of our tour to be spent in Leningrad, leaving very little time for the usual run of visits to famous places. To some this may have been disappointing, but to others in the group, including Ronald, who still, in spite of all remedial treatment, were suffering the distressing symptoms of the virulent bug caught in Moscow – Scotland could not come too soon.

On the first day of our arrival we were herded into a bus and taken to the Hermitage. It is common knowledge that to savour in full the dazzling interior of this vast museum calls for some considerable time – not just a fleeting visit but many long hours and even days. We, however, were to experience the alternative.

We hurried at full speed from room to room; barely halting to admire the paintings, statues, rich carvings, the malachite pillars, the bronze and gold on the doors – all rich and wonderful and barely remembered. I recollect stopping to admire the portrait of the Duke of Wellington in the Hall of the Generals – only to find myself left behind the others and having to run to join them.

There was a vague memory when ascending the grand staircase of having been there before, climbing the same steps holding my father's hand.

St Isaac's, under the great Golden Dome, was also worth a visit. In 1972 no services were held there. Beautiful as the interior is, it was neither a church nor a museum and only served as a sad reminder of other times when people of all classes came to pray and listen to the exquisite singing of the choir.

Another day with two of our friends we set off by the metro to the famous 'Hotel Astoria' where we were told that the 'Berezka' shop attached to the hotel offered the best selection of souvenirs. There I bought a few articles including the ever popular lacquered boxes depicting attractive Russian scenes. Our two friends, having also purchased some gifts, decided to return to the 'Russia' but were apprehensive about travelling by themselves, as not being familiar with the Russian alphabet they would be unable to recognise the name of their station. Ronald, being acquainted with the Cyrillic alphabet and having a smattering of Russian, decided to escort them, while I, still intent on buying another picture, set off on my own along the Nevski Prospect in search of the shop which I had been told was reputed to have a rich selection of fine paintings.

After the warmth and sunshine of Sochi, St Petersburg was chilly with a hint of approaching autumn. Clouds like torn rags drifted across a pale sky. A colourless mass of pedestrians kept moving to and fro, all intent on their own business. There was a dreary sameness especially in the clothes of the women. I saw neither style nor anything to admire. 'Where had the brilliance, light and colour of this golden city vanished?' I asked myself.

One of my nieces who was born and bred in St Petersburg and now lives in Sweden gave me her impression of St Petersburg after she had paid a visit there in order to find the house and street where she was born and to glean some information regarding the death of her father, executed by Stalin.

'St Petersburg,' she said, 'was like a beautiful woman who had been badly beaten.' It was an apt description. Magnificent and beautiful as still are the palaces, museums and churches drawing masses of tourists from the hated West whose money is so necessary to uphold the tottering economy, the aura of majestic elegance is no longer there. Although the two world wars had undoubtedly left their mark, it is as nothing when compared to the devastation and suffering endured for seventy years under communism.

From the very start of the revolution, Lenin set out to destroy completely the very soul of Russia and what he left unfinished Stalin completed with sadistic efficiency. After hijacking democracy, the calamitous October Revolution of 1917 blighted one of the great cultures in Europe. Had it not taken place, Russia today would have been to the fore or at least on a par culturally and economically with her neighbours in the west and not reduced to begging as she is doing today while I am writing these lines.

Yet, how many of the Western intellectuals firmly believed that the Revolution was necessary for Russia! Brilliant statesmen in high places and writers such as George Bernard Shaw waxed eloquent in their praise of communism. Malcolm Muggeridge, too, was an ardent supporter, but underwent a rapid change of heart after a sojourn in Russia. In recent years there has been a tendency, especially since Gorbachev's *Perestroika*, to exonerate Lenin from all blame while condemning Stalin's excesses: 'Remember the teaching of our great leader, Comrade Vladimir Ilyich Lenin,' cried Gorbachev.

What I remember is the well-known fact that at the start of his reign, Lenin issued a secret order to deal mercilessly with all opposition. It was during this time that the Royal Family were butchered and millions tortured, executed and sent to prisons including the ancient Solovetski Monastery on the White Sea, reputed later to be the worst prison camp in the whole of Russia. I myself, during Lenin's time, when fourteen years old, vividly remember watching a group of men including a young student in his grey uniform being led to their execution in the woods. As far as Stalin is concerned, it was a case of the disciple excelling his master. In so doing, he succeeded in reducing most of Soviet society to a quivering mass of terror and panic.

As I continued my way on Nevsky Prospect, I became aware of curious glances directed at me now and again by passing pedestrians and remembered being told that foreigners were usually recognised as such by the clothes they wore and especially by their footwear. It was difficult to find in Russia good shoes, clothing and things which we in the West take for granted.

It came to me with a feeling of guilt, that here perhaps were survivors, friends and relatives of those who perished in the epic siege of St Petersburg (Leningrad) – the greatest and most terrible siege in modern times – a horror that lasted 900 days and claimed the lives of a million people, including my uncle and his wife and son, who died from starvation.

I was living in India at the time and although the threat from Japan was always present, life on the whole was pleasant and free from care. There were various functions taking place such as dances, tennis parties, mah-jongg drives, all in aid of war funds. Private dinners and mah-jongg tea parties were likewise exchanged between our own friends. Little did I think while playing mah-jongg and enjoying the rich pastries and cakes, that in distant war-torn Russia, my relatives were dying of starvation. It was only after my return to Scotland with our two young sons at the end of the war that I was able to get in touch with my relatives in Finland and learn through them of the tragic deaths of so many members of my family in Archangel and St Petersburg.

Especially poignant was the fate of Seryozha, my young step-uncle. He was more like an older brother, a boy of a gentle disposition who used to join in all our ploys, whether the gilding of the walnuts for the Christmas tree or assisting in the production of a play and one who kept us spellbound when listening to him reading from some Russian classic as we gathered round the table on a winter's night.

After his marriage in the early Twenties he moved with his wife to St Petersburg where he became curator of a museum. At the start of the war and before the siege began Seryozha and his family had the chance to leave St Petersburg but feeling it was his duty to preserve the objects under his care he decided to stay.

Seryozha was the first to die of starvation. He was followed by his son Yurie – a brilliant sixteen-year-old student. His fellow students who tried to save him placed Yurie on a sledge and pulled it to the hospital, but he died on arrival. Masha, Seryozha's wife, died some days later and the three of them were buried together in a common grave in the Piskarevsky Cemetery where a million victims of the siege lie in common graves.

Nina, the twelve-year-old daughter, was the sole survivor. She was rescued by a wonderful couple, a man and wife who dedicated their lives to rescuing orphaned children. With loving care they not only sheltered and fed them but saw that they were educated and appreciative of the arts by taking them to galleries, plays and concerts. 'Somewhere in this city lives Nina,' I kept repeating to myself as I continued walking, 'but where, where can it be? How I would love to meet her.'

I found the shop on Nevsky Prospect. Inside, as promised, there was a rich and varied collection of prints, etchings and paintings displayed on every wall.

Although not an expert I still enjoyed just browsing around looking for something that might catch my eye. A painting depicting an ancient scene in Moscow caught my attention. I was drawn to the warm hues of green, gold and red and tempted to buy it. It was one of a row hanging on the wall in front of which was a long counter divided for some reason by a cord.

Approaching the young woman standing there, appraising me with cold indifference. I enquired, 'How much is this picture?'

'I don't know,' she rejoined with a bored glance at the painting. 'It is not on my part of the counter. The girl responsible for the other side is not on duty just now.'

'Could you not sell it for her?' I persisted. 'The painting is for sale, is it not?'

'Yes,' she agreed, 'but not today. Call again in two days. She will probably be back by then.'

'I shall be leaving for Scotland and not likely to return,' I pointed out in the hope that a little persuasion might cause her to relent, but with the same indifference she shrugged her shoulders and turned away. Infuriating as it was, there was nothing one could do against such gross stupidity.

I was, however, rewarded by the unexpected find of a totally different painting, more pleasing than the one I could not buy. Whoever the artist was he must have been someone from the North as this picture of a village was similar to one I knew so well, situated on the shores of the Dvina directly opposite our house. I immediately recognised the wintry scene, the snowdrifts, the small northern horse pulling a load of hay, the peasants' cottages, snow-laden roofs, frosted windows, nearby a bare solitary tree. I was reminded of how, long ago in the early spring, my playmates and I would set off on our skis across the frozen river to the willow woods behind the village. There we gathered the willow sprays with their silvery catkins which, later decorated with ribbons and artificial flowers, were proudly carried to church on Palm Sunday.

The young man who sold me the painting was a far more pleasant being than the sulky girl at the other counter. We had a long and friendly chat together. On hearing about my background he displayed a great interest in Scotland and was not afraid to ask many questions or express the hope that he might one day visit our part of the world. Prior to leaving we shook hands and I departed with my precious picture to board the metro for my return to the hotel. Some time later, back in Scotland, the two paintings – one from Moscow, the other from St Petersburg – were hung up on the walls of our home, each one serving to remind me of a scene from my childhood.

Our stay in St Petersburg was now drawing to a close. Another day and a night and we would board the 'plane for Scotland. I was determined to contact my relatives, but up to date the various activities prevented us from going off on our own.

The following day, after an unusual journey by hydrofoil we visited Peterhof (Peter's Palace), one of the most prestigious and beautiful palaces lying on the shores of the Gulf of Finland, some twenty-nine kilometres from St Petersburg.

The magnificence of Peterhof is impressive, more so than any other place I visited in Russia. It was there while strolling around admiring the restored palaces, pavilions and fountains that I fully realised how great was the resilience and undaunted courage of the Russian people.

Hitler's army with their inherent thoroughness burned, looted and destroyed all the palaces and parks in the vicinity of St Petersburg, and none more than Peterhof, where only a burned-out shell was left by the retreating army.

It was thought at the time that nothing could ever be the same again, but the inhabitants refused to admit defeat and with victory in sight courageously began the restoration. They came from all walks of life – architects, builders, workers, soldiers, artists and students.

Life in post-war Russia was chaotic. The scarcity of food and all other basic needs was enormous. There were also the ever-present sinister figures of Stalin and his successors in the background. Yet, each one with loving dedication in the face of all difficulties toiled over the next decades until the restoration was complete and out of the dust and rubble the palaces and parks appeared in all their former glory. Such transformation was nothing short of a miracle. In 1973 Peterhof was decorated with the Order of the Sign of Honour for this amazing achievement.

Inside the main palace the restoration is likewise complete. Peter the Great's study, with his desk, candlesticks and books is just the same as it was in his time, as are all the other rooms. It is impossible not to experience a sense of humility, when observing how much care and attention had been expended on the smallest detail from the pen and books in Peter's study, to the delicate ornaments in the 'Divan Room'. Guards stationed in each room kept a watchful eye on the visitors moving from room to room. Special attention is paid to the parquet flooring laid out in beautiful designs. No one is allowed to step on to it without previously donning thick felt slippers provided by the attendants.

After leaving the palace we spent some time strolling in the park or sitting on a form admiring the cascading fountains with the golden sculptures decorating the steps.

The whole visit was a pleasant unique experience still remembered over the years. We travelled on our return journey by bus and after an interesting run through the outskirts of St Petersburg duly arrived at our hotel in time for dinner.

After dinner our group set off to attend a talk on 'Friendship'. This was a golden opportunity for us to slip away in a final attempt to find my cousin. We were encouraged by the experience of our son, George, in Russia away back during the reign of Nikita Khrushchev, a period known as 'The Time of the Thaw'.

One afternoon during a spell in India in the early Sixties we unexpectedly received a call from Delhi enquiring if we had a son named George Fraser in Moscow. Astonished and alarmed we asked ourselves 'Why is George in Moscow – what is he up to – is he in trouble?' His cheerful voice, however, coming clearly over from Moscow, dispelled our fears.

It transpired that, during that time of tolerance, a cultural delegation comprising the first British student group ever to visit the USSR was sent from Scotland to Russia. Its membership was drawn from the then Scottish Union of Students representing all the Universities of Scotland and included our son George who was reading law at Edinburgh University. From all accounts they were warmly welcomed and entertained in Russia, attended places of interest, visited other towns including Kiev, held lively parties and generally enjoyed themselves.

While in Leningrad, George found Ulitza Marata where my cousin Victoria lived and called on her. Although astonished, she was delighted to discover who George was and on the following day held a party in his honour attended by all the members of the family. A friendly neighbour acted as an interpreter and spent the evening translating all the reminiscences and questions. Although life was difficult, there was an abundance of food and vodka on the table and everyone had joined in to make the party a success. It was a warm friendly gathering, accompanied by toasts in vodka and champagne and culminating in George tape-recording all the messages to be passed on to absent relatives and especially to their sister Olga in America.

Now full of optimism we began to arrange the gifts we brought from Scotland. There were several sweaters, cardigans, blouses, pairs of socks, stockings, as well as coffee and sweets, but not wishing to attract attention we decided to pack a holdall and put the smaller articles such as coffee and sweets in Ronald's pocket. As our departure the following day for Scotland was not due until after lunch we hoped that Victoria or someone else could call at the hotel and pick up the remaining gifts.

After leaving the hotel we took the metro to the station which Ronald reckoned was the nearest to Ulitza Marata. On arrival, however, not being certain if we were going in the right direction I stopped a young girl to ask her if she could help us. She answered briefly 'Follow me' and walked a few steps in front, obviously not wishing to be seen in our company. On reaching a junction, she raised her arm indicating we had to turn left and then she continued walking without a backward glance.

We were now in Ulitza Marata, a bleak street of ancient tenement buildings. We had no difficulty in finding the block in which Victoria lived. Inside the gloomy entrance a rickety lift took us to the third floor, where, in the narrow hall facing us, was a large dark door. I rang the bell. The door was opened by a tall, good-looking young man dressed in a track suit bearing the name of a club.

Inside was a long corridor on the right side of which could be seen three doors, each representing a single large room housing a family. Straight ahead at the end of the corridor we noticed a communal kitchen and next to it another door which I presumed led to the toilet. On our left, beside a window, was a table with a telephone. The young man did not appear to be enthralled by our presence. Somewhat unnerved by his unsmiling countenance I said to him, 'We are from Scotland. It is possible for us to see Victoria Aleksandrovna? I am her cousin.'

'Victoria Aleksandrovna,' he replied pointing to the first door which appeared to be locked, 'is away to the country with her family.'

Disappointed and put out by the young man's attitude I continued hopefully, 'Do you by any chance have the address of Victoria's brother, Evgenie Alexsandrovich, or perhaps his telephone number?'

Obviously exasperated, he answered shortly: 'He moved recently – I don't know where to.'

Although upset by his open hostility, having gone so far I still went on: 'Is it possible then to get in touch with their step-sister Nora?'

'She lives in the outskirts of the town,' he replied with undisguised irritation in his voice, but to my surprise added, 'I could 'phone her if you wish.' He did 'phone but after a short conversation put down the receiver. 'She does not wish to speak to you, and as for me,' he continued, 'I cannot do any more for you – I am already compromised by being involved in your visit.' We, I was beginning to realise, must be 'The Untouchables', perhaps the carriers of the plague, a source of great danger to be avoided at all costs!

Ronald, whose Russian was limited, at first remained silent, but understanding enough to be astonished by such a blatant display of hostility, now turned to me. '*Poidyom*' ('Let's go') he said.

We placed the gifts we had brought on the table and moved towards the exit but with that the door adjoining my cousin's opened and a small, elderly woman appeared, who, it transpired later, was the young man's mother. 'I feel,' she said, 'you have to know the truth. I am quite old and do not fear any longer. Your cousin Victoria has been subjected to a frightening experience. It so happened that being a good engineer, she was offered as a reward, a permit to travel abroad, but prior to leaving had to complete answers to a questionnaire. One of the questions was "Do you have relatives abroad?" Knowing that the truth would be a barrier to her journey she foolishly wrote "None" being quite unaware that the authorities knew all along that she had a sister in America and a cousin in Scotland. The K.G.B. swooped down and told her she had lied. The trip was cancelled and she was warned that any contact with the West would be severely punished. This would apply not only to herself but to all members of her family.' Knowing through my letter when I was likely to call on her she simply left the house.

While this unhappy conversation was taking place the telephone rang. The old lady lifted the receiver and I heard her say, 'Yes she is still here and you can speak to her.' I took the telephone and discovered that the caller was Nora, my cousin's step-sister. 'How is my sister, Olga?' she enquired.

'Your sister is well and happy – we correspond with each other,' I replied.

'Tell her,' Nora continued, sobbing as she spoke, 'tell her that we love her and will never forget her but tell her also that she must never write to us, tell her to forget us and please Jenya, abandon any further attempts to contact us, do not come near us just leave us alone.'

By now, also upset, I could only answer, 'I will do as you ask me – I wish you well.' There was nothing more to say. I thanked the old lady for having told us the true facts of this sorry tale, exchanged a few words, asked her to give Victoria our presents, pass on our love, and left the house.

Little was said as we wound our way along the dreary Ulitza Marata. We had been devastated, not only by the heartbreak of being unable to meet my relatives but by the stark realisation that in high positions in government there was a mob of gangsters who could terrorise, threaten and punish completely innocent and helpless members of society.

It was a great relief to be back in the hotel. On the landing of the floor where our bedroom was situated, sitting at her desk was a pleasant young woman who held the keys of all the rooms. I asked her for our key. Smiling as she handed it over she enquired, 'Where did you learn to speak such pure Russian?'

'In the Mariyanskaya Gymnazia, in Archangel, where I was born and brought up,' I replied.

'Ah! Archangel,' she sighed, 'I was there last summer. How beautiful it was, that lovely river, the white nights, the scent of the wild cherry blossom.'

'Yes,' I agreed. 'The summers were always lovely – but you must know that I can never see them.' She looked up and perhaps seeing I was upset did not answer.

We retreated to our bedroom where, after sitting for some time in silence, we began to pack our boxes for the return journey next day. While thus engaged we heard a knock on the door. I became alarmed thinking that perhaps someone from the K.G.B. was after me. Too afraid to go to the door I said to Ronald, 'You open it.' He did so – and there, standing holding a beautiful bouquet of flowers, was the friendly 'key lady'. 'Please,' she said, handing over the flowers, 'give this to your wife with our love.' This I believe was the brightest moment of the whole trip. 'Russia is not dead. Russia lives on,' I said to myself.

The next day a bus took us to the airport where we duly boarded the 'plane for Glasgow. Soon we were up in the clouds with Russia far behind us and after an uneventful flight of some three and a half hours were back in Scotland.

I do not know if it was the relief of being back and away from the grey skies of Leningrad, but as I came down the steps of the 'plane everything around me appeared to be flooded in the brightest of sunshine. A piper in full regalia, standing nearby, was playing a welcoming air. Jean turned to me. 'I could kiss the hem of his kilt,' she said. We said goodbye to her and John and the friends who had brightened our stay in Russia and, although still fondly remembered, we never met again.

Outside the airport our son Michael with his young wife Jennifer and our baby grandson were awaiting us with Ronald's beloved Citroen. 'Well, how did you like your old Russia?' Michael asked me.

I was noncommital. 'It is a long story. You will hear about it later,' I replied. Ronald's comment was short. 'I am still suffering,' he said. He was referring to the legacy from Moscow, the bug which had affected the majority of the group and pursued them to the very end of their stay in Russia. We had no knowledge of what may have cured our fellow travellers, but in Ronald's case all the prescriptions and visits to the doctor and chemist proved of no avail until one day when I was preparing lunch he picked up a tattered copy of *Tried Favourites*, a book much loved by housewives from the days of Queen Victoria and bequeathed to me by my mother. In the appendix amongst the various cures he read the following: 'For summer diarrhoea pick three strawberry leaves, wash thoroughly, chew and swallow!' He went to the garden, found the leaves and followed the instructions. The result was nothing short of a miracle!

It was good to be back to the familiar places, the streets, the shops, to meet old friends, to start afresh the daily routine of our lives. There was no desire ever to return to Russia. As far as I was concerned Russia was finished. The loving gift of flowers presented to me on the eve of our departure had kindled a spark of hope – soon to go out. There was nothing whatever to pull me back. I have to thank my lucky star for the gift of a Scots mother but for whom my brother and I would not have been able to escape from Russia and settle in Scotland, a country I consider, after many sojourns in other lands, to be the best in the world.

And yet in spite of all that I say, why does this yearning for something long since lost never leave me? It is my belief that this nostalgia haunts most Russians, who, no matter how well they settle down in foreign lands, cannot forget their motherland.

During my long sojourn in India it was possible when flying home after the war, on leave or returning to India, to break our journey in Paris and spend a few days with my Russian cousin and her husband. They ran a profitable little factory, creating powder compacts and jewel boxes, hand-painted in beautiful designs and selling well in post-war Paris.

Those fleeting visits were always a source of pleasure as we got to know many of the Russian emigrés, who had fled to France after the 1918 revolution to escape the tragic débâcle of the civil war. They all loved France and her people, who in turn accepted and liked the Russians, but when the usual gatherings took place around my cousin's hospitable table, accompanied by vodka and zakuskis the theme was only Russia. We listened for hours on end to all the reminiscences – some sad, some humorous but always touched by a sense of loss for a world to which they never could return.

I remember meeting an old Cossack in a prestigious restaurant which he ran in the heart of Paris. On discovering that I could talk in Russian, he remained standing beside our table where he had placed a delicious selection of Russian dishes, for which I may add in the passing we paid quite sweetly! 'I,' he said in mournful tones, 'have a French wife and daughters who barely know a word of Russian. At times when I feel sad, I take a bottle of vodka and go into a quiet corner of the garden and there I'll sit alone and think about our village, the friends I knew and my father's cottage with the cherry tree beside it!'

It is not only the exiles who cherish this love for the land of their birth. Foreigners who lived in Russia have likewise felt this fascination, as did my mother, a true Scot, who, when reminiscing about her time there always maintained that, in spite of a tragic outcome, she loved Russia and her people and would never have left it had it not been for the horrors of the revolution.

I have an old English friend born and bought up in Archangel, but educated by English tutors. He, like many more, had fled with his family to the safety of Britain's shores, never to return.

In his letters he tells me that even after a long sojourn in England he still cannot overcome his longing for Russia. 'At times,' he adds, 'when walking on the streets of London, lost in my memories, I will sing an old Russian song – to the great astonishment of the passers-by!'

What is the secret of this elusive charm? There is no answer. The great Russian writer, N.V. Gogol, has a passage in his famous narrative *Dead Souls*, where he asks the same question: 'What is this power that lies hidden in you? Everything in you is open, empty, flat. Your lowly towns are stuck like dots upon your plains, nothing to beguile the eye, but what is this incomprehensible force that draws me to you? Why does your mournful song, carried along your whole length and breadth from sea to sea, echo incessantly in my ears? What is there in that song that calls and sobs and clutches at my heart? Russia! What do you want of me – what is that mysterious hidden bond between us?'

Chapter 2

THE MISSING YEARS

ONE RAINY DAY in late September, while engaged in creating some form of order out of a large heap of papers and letters accumulated throughout the years, I came across my own scribblings compiled during our stay of four years in Thailand.

We were living at the time some forty kilometres from Bangkok near a village called Rangsit, surrounded by a great expanse of emerald green rice fields, where Ronald was engaged in running a jute mill for the Ministry of Finance of the Government of Thailand.

During the weekend breaks it was our custom to set off for Bangkok where we explored the various temples, palaces and places of interest with which the beautiful 'Venice of the East' is so richly endowed. There was also the occasional film to see and at the end of these outings an excellent dinner – usually in the Hotel Erawan, which nowadays, I am told, no longer exists. Trips to the outlying small towns and villages were likewise rewarding – especially the delightful seaside resort of Pataya, unspoiled in those far off days, where we experienced the pleasure of water skiing.

The weekends were always joyful but for me, during the week with Ronald engrossed in his work, the hours passed slowly. The excursions each Monday to the Bangkok market with my little cook Somana were a pleasant change as were the visits to a kind and hospitable Russian lady whom I met at a reception in the British Consulate. The odd invitations to cocktail parties given by business associates and our managing director were also welcome and helped to brighten our daily round.

Our modern Thai house, although not as spacious as we might have liked, was comfortable, but the air-conditioning was only installed in the bedrooms. Unlike Bengal, when a break of cool weather lasting three months brought a welcome relief from the steamy heat, in Bangkok the seasons never varied – it was always hot!

With Ronald's departure to the office, I formed the habit after lunch of retreating to our pleasant air-conditioned bedroom where, lying on top of the bed, I would spend the afternoon reading. A great boon was the excellent

Bangkok library housing a wonderful collection of books on various topics which helped to while away many a lonesome hour.

At times, when tired of reading, I enjoyed watching the constant activities of a pair of sparrows, nesting in the eaves of the house close to the window. The stamina of these tiny creatures in procreating their species in such quick succession never ceased to amaze me. I became addicted to watching the endless bustle of our little feathered tenants – the arrival of the fledglings, the total dedication of the parents to their young, soon to leave their nest, and the happy round commencing once again.

To Ronald, however, the description of my observations fell on barren ground. 'Rather than wasting your time in spying on the love life of the sparrows,' he had remarked, 'you would be better employed in writing about your childhood in Russia, for our sons. The boys would like it.' Such a thought had never entered my head but now, following my husband's advice, I began to write, though only when the mood took over or the sudden recollection of some almost forgotten incident would compel me to snatch a pen and write it down before it vanished from my memory.

Four years on, by now retired from the East and settled in Edinburgh, we were much occupied purchasing a house, accompanied by the usual labour involved in redecorating and general improvements. There were likewise family affairs – weddings, the arrival of grandchildren and over all the ever repetitive chores in running a home which left little time to indulge in any writing.

Yet on that morning when I came across the faded bundle of paper with my almost forgotten scribbling I was suddenly overcome by a deep desire to continue.

Yes, I promised myself, I will tell my sons about the house which once stood on the shores of the mighty Dvina, the people who lived there, their hopes and dreams, the happy or sad events that took place before and during my childhood.

I will describe the unique and beautiful garden with the lovely trees and flowers, the lake and the fantastic summer house above it – straight out of a fairy tale: a garden designed and created by my talented grandmother – a place of delight and enchantment – enjoyed by young and old, doomed to vanish from the face of the earth along with the house and the people in it during the darkest hours of Russia's history.

I wrote over many long years ignoring the passing hours, never dreaming that one day the account of my childhood in Russia would be published and read in many parts of the world.

One morning in the late autumn of 1972 when our unhappy experience in Russia, like an unpleasant dream, was almost forgotten, I received a letter which, to my astonishment, was sent from Leningrad (St Petersburg) by my cousin Evgenie.

Dear Jenya,

I have only recently discovered that you were in Leningrad and tried to get in touch with us. I cannot tell you how bitterly disappointed I am to have missed your visit, especially so as it may never occur again. Victoria may have had her reasons to leave for her cotttage in the country, but there was nothing to prevent my step-sister Nora from giving you my address and telephone number. Believe me, had I but known that you were here I would have run all the way to meet you if only for a few minutes. There was so much we could have talked about, especially concerning your dear father, who as you know lived with us after your departure for Scotland.

I am so angry with Nora for not mentioning your visit until a few days ago. I can't forgive her – our relations since then have become quite cold.

I trust, dear Jenya, it is not too much to expect an answer to my letter. I'm enclosing my address in the hope that you may drop a few lines to me.

With love and best wishes,

Your cousin

Evgenie.

I did answer and from that time began a correspondence between us lasting until his death many years later.

It so happened that in the year 1920, after my mother fled to Scotland with my brother and me (having been forced to leave our sick father behind), we were for many months out of touch with Archangel and even later, when we succeeded in making contact and began a steady exchange of letters with our father, there were still so many events outwith our knowledge which had happened after we left. My cousin Evgenie, a talented writer, in his letters conveys with great clarity the scenes of various happenings – the struggles for existence, their way of life, described with a lively sense of humour or profound pathos.

Recently, having re-read his letters, I decided to translate some extracts as it is my belief that there are very few people left who can still remember and describe the early days of the terrible Twenties in the aftermath of the Bolshevik revolution.

Evgenie and I were both named after our babushka (grandmother), his name being the male version of Evgeniya (Eugenie), but to avoid confusion I will refer to him by his full name of Evgenie instead of 'Jenya' as we were both called.

Before me lies a letter dated November 1972 describing the event which took place in late October of 1920, an event that might have changed the whole course of my life and that of my mother and brother. Evgenie wrote:

I remember that day so well. My parents had brought me along to say 'Goodbye' and we had all gathered in Uncle Gherman's bedroom. I remember you standing beside me at the window waving to the 'Gang' who had arrived at the gate and were waiting to escort you to the ship. Ghermosha [my young brother Gherman] was sitting on the edge of the bed where my Uncle was lying, holding Ghermosha's hand and telling him something.

The house was strangely silent. Nothing was the same since Babushka's departure to join Dedushka [Grandpa] in exile. Uncle Yura was staying with his old nurse in a village across the river. Uncle Seryozha was away showing the town to the two young teachers who had arrived from Leningrad and were accommodated in the drawing-room. Perhaps you may remember that later Uncle Seryozha married one of the girls, named Masha, and went to live in Leningrad.

The samovar was singing on the table. My mother and Aunt Nelly were sitting beside it talking quietly. Cousin Marina was also there. My father, in a restless manner, was pacing up and down the room. Over all there was a heavy sadness, an awareness that the inevitable goodbyes were drawing nearer with their tears and anguish.

Suddenly Aleksander Aleksandrovich, Ghermosha's godfather, distressed and out of breath, burst into the room. Apparently he had called at the ship only to find that it was on the point of leaving and that you had not yet arrived.

The captain was furious and it was only after Aleksander's desperate pleading that he agreed to wait for another half-hour but not a minute longer.

It turned out to be, as perhaps you, Jenya, will remember, Aunt Nelly's fault as in the morning after Arsyenie set off for the dock with the cart carrying your luggage and duly delivered it to the ship, Aunt Nelly followed to check if everything was in order. There, while talking to the captain, she was reminded that the ship was due to sail at 14.00 hours which she wrongly took to be 4 p.m. instead of 2 p.m.

Aleksandr, who discovered this terrible mistake had run all the way to the house and arrived utterly exhausted. Pandemonium broke out – hurried farewells, poignant blessings and the room emptied. It was decided during these short seconds that Aunt Nelly with my mother were to hurry for the tramcar while you and Ghermosha accompanied by your gang, ran along the road by the river and whoever was first would beg the captain to wait for the others.

I hurried to the window and saw the gang headed by Petya Skroznikov, known to be a fast runner, with you behind him, racing on the river front and then vanish out of sight.

I returned and sat down on the bed beside Uncle Gherman, who remained silent with his arm thrown over his face. Aleksandr Aleksandrovich stayed on talking quietly with my father.

After a while, Uncle asked me to go to the balcony from where I would see the ship passing by but when I got there I found Cousin Marina waving a towel to the ship disappearing behind the Island of Solombala. She told me she had seen you and Ghermosa quite clearly waving back to her. I had just missed you by a few seconds. Shortly, your friend Petya arrived at the house and gave a vivid description of what took place aboard the ship. Petya had been the first to run up the gangway with you, Jenya, behind him, but to their horror there was no sign of Aunt Nelly. The infuriated captain immediately ordered his men to throw your baggage on to the dock. At this point, Petya went on, Jenya burst into tears and going down on her knees begged the captain to wait for just a few more minutes. In this she was joined by all the other passengers and the members of the gang all pleading in one voice on Jenya's behalf until to everybody's great relief someone espied Aunt Nelly and my mother walking calmly and unhurriedly towards the ship and as Petya added 'as if the two of them were out on a Sunday stroll'.

Soon everything fell into place. The ship began to move, at first slowly and then with ever increasing speed. The gang ran alongside with you and Ghermosha waving to them but were soon left behind.

That is how I remember, dear Jenya, the sad day of your departure. In the evening my mother and I went home, but my father and Aleksandr decided to spend the night with Uncle Gherman.

The next morning we returned to the house to find a group of workmen had arrived and were measuring all the rooms for the purpose of dividing each room so as to accommodate the students and staff from the neighbouring Technical School.

The house was requisitioned by the government and when the notice was served it was decided that after your departure Uncle Gherman would move over to stay with us.

Now, Arsyenie harnessed the horse, and gently lifting my Uncle carried him down to the carriage. There, surrounded by all his belongings and accompanied by my father, Uncle Gherman left his home, never to return.

It was a short journey to our house, for as you will remember, we lived in the nearby Uspenskaya Ulitza, named after the church of the same name which was later removed and the street renamed Proletarskaya.

Our house, two-storeyed and rather bleak, was similar to many more in that style. It was, however, spacious and being rented was not liable to be requisitioned as were so many of the better houses.

I was the eldest of the four children followed by my sister Victoria and brother Aleksandr, better known as 'Shurick', and much later by my sister Olga who appeared on the scene a year after you left during the most difficult period of our lives when food and even the barest necessities were almost unobtainable.

When Uncle Gherman arrived at our house it was decided that he and I would share a bedroom. This worked out very well, for as time went by a mutual affection developed between us which, without unduly flattering myself, I believe helped to ease the pain of missing his own children.

At times when sitting talking to my Uncle, I used to ask myself 'Why was it that those eyes so blue and clear could not see the light of day?' Yet in spite of his sad fate he was always cheerful and possessed a lively sense of humour, liked to sing to himself, or make up little verses about his numerous friends. His sense of hearing was amazing and by listening to the footsteps coming up the stairs he could always identify the visitor.

One of the many friends who used to visit Uncle was Anna Osipovna, the widow of our Babushka's brother, Uncle Vanya. She was, you may remember, a small woman aptly named 'Osa' [meaning 'the Wasp']. The first two letters of her patronymic, Osipovna, may have had some bearing on her name, but it was also very apt for she possessed a sharp tongue and quick, all-seeing eyes. Osa was a compulsive chain smoker who found it difficult to live without a cigarette and was known to give up her ration card for bread in exchange for some tobacco.

Uncle Gherman also enjoyed smoking cigarettes which he skilfully rolled himself. On his bedside table there was always a container with tobacco and paper – a great temptation to Osa, who surreptitiously used to help herself to Uncle's tobacco.

I recollect watching an amusing scene which took place one afternoon. Osa was sitting beside my Uncle and telling him an interesting tale, meanwhile quietly pinching his tobacco, not realising that Uncle possessed excellent hearing.

When she came to the end of her story, I heard my Uncle say, 'What you have described to me, my dear Osa, was certainly remarkable – but did you at the same time have to steal my tobacco?' 'Oh how could you think, Gherman, that I would do such a disgraceful thing to you?' was the indignant reply.

After this incident, whenever Uncle heard her footsteps, he would exclaim to me, 'Here she comes, Evgenie. Please quickly hide my tobacco.'

Meanwhile, back in the house other events were taking place. Both my step-uncles, Yura and Seryozha, were presented with a notice to leave. Cousin Marina had already left for Finland. She being deaf had to be escorted to Leningrad and on arrival put on a train for Helsinki, where she was met by Aunt Olga [her mother] to join all her numerous sisters and her one brother.

She called at our house on the eve of her departure to say 'Goodbye' to us all, weeping bitterly when embracing Uncle Gherman, for as you know, she spent many years with Babushka and the family. She was especially fond of Uncle Gherman because he used to tell her stories.

One day, soon after Marina left, young Petya Scroznikov rushed in to tell us that the house was on fire. We immediately ran to the scene. On arrival we found a large crowd of people milling around. Yura and Seryozha were running in and out of the house trying to save some of the contents. Aunt Marga and her husband Dmitri were also there dragging out pictures and icons. My parents with great difficulty succeeded in rescuing the lifesize miracle icon of St Nicholas, much treasured by Babushka. I was not allowed to go in and could only watch some strange 'helpers' who were engaged in removing from the house various articles which were never seen again.

Smoke and flames were belching out of one of the windows but no one could tell why the fire started. Some thought it may have been sabotage, others blamed faulty wiring. Babushka's graceful palms and precious rare plants were dragged on to the balcony and from there thrown on to the roadway only to be trampled underfoot and destroyed.

The timely arrival of the fire brigade saved the house from complete destruction. Later, it was roughly repaired, the balcony facing the river removed and the damaged walls covered by planks. The end result presented a picture of a house that bore no resemblance to the original.

For some time the rooms remained empty, but later students moved in and later still the house was turned into a hospital for children.

Shortly after the fire the horse was taken away. Arsyenie left to work elsewhere. With the passing of time the empty stables were removed as was the coach house with all the various carriages and sledges. Vassili, the old gardener, who had spent a life time cherishing the garden and who used to chase us if we dared to pick a flower, likewise saw no purpose in staying on and left for his village.

Do you remember, Jenya, how we liked to play in the garden? You, I still see as a round-faced girl, with brown curly hair and always smiling. You used to say, when my parents brought me along, 'Come with us Jenchick. Let's play in the garden'.

The garden was a huge attraction with its high summerhouse and panes of coloured glass through which we liked to see the trees and flowers in different hues. Best of all was the pond and the raft. The three of us used to go sailing around, ducking under the overhanging branches of the trees. You were always the leader. What stories you used to tell Ghermosha and me – 'This the great Amazon river, Red Indians are hiding in the bushes with their bows and arrows'. I could not swim and was terrified of drowning but you always assured me: 'Don't be afraid Jenchick – I will save you, I'm a good swimmer.'

It was Yura's dog, the pointer 'Kieng', always following us that spoiled it all that day when he came rushing behind us and leapt on to the raft, just as we had pushed off. The raft turned over and we were pitched into the water. You immediately caught me and, true to your promise, saved my life. Do you remember how angry Babushka was when we arrived soaking wet at the house? The raft was immediately broken up and burned in the pechka. That was the end of all the expeditions to the Amazon!

After you left, I, with my playmates, at times visited the deserted garden. In the pond there still remained small inedible fish, smelling of stagnant water. We enjoyed the fishing and feeding an eager audience of cats, but each time I went there I was conscious of a deep, haunting sadness on seeing how rapidly everything had decayed and vanished and preferred instead to play beside the river where I soon learned to swim.

How are you dear Jenya? (writes my cousin in a letter dated February 1973). It is quite a while since last I heard from you. I keep looking in my post-box each day, but find nothing. We read you are having a severe winter, with frosts and snowstorms and I trust you are all keeping well.

Here things are much the same. We had a visit from Victoria and her husband the other night and sat around the table beside the samovar talking of many things. Victoria is getting very deaf, but still looks remarkably well.

I have been going over some of the letters written many years back. It is rather strange, but when reading about certain events I have the impression that it has all happened quite recently.

Most vivid is the memory of the arrival of the long-awaited letter from Aunt Nelly. You left in October of 1920, but it wasn't until the spring of 1921 that we received the glad news of your safe arrival in Scotland. For months we had worried and poor Uncle Gherman fretted his heart out wondering if you did succeed in reaching Norway from Murmansk. You just can't imagine what great joy that letter brought to us all.

From what I can gather the whole journey was a succession of amazing coincidences. It was fortunate that the *Sever* [*The North*] could not return to Archangel on account of the usual freeze-up of the Dvina and in this way the captain kindly allowed you to live aboard his ship in Murmansk. You were also lucky in finding a dining-room which provided a daily meal of soup and kasha. What could only be described as nothing less than a miracle was that when, after a hopeless search for a boat to take you to Norway, you were resigned to returning to Archangel, Aunt Nelly and your travelling companion Mme Ankirova had the good fortune to meet the young skipper of a trawler, an old acquaintance of Madame Ankirova. He told them that he had been commissioned to take two important commissars to the Island of Vardo and who, after hearing of your plight, kindly offered all of you passages on his ship. Even stranger was that on arrival in Vardo, after surviving a terrible storm, it was only Aunt Nelly with you, Ghermosha and Madame Ankirova who were allowed to go ashore and the luckless trawler with the two important passengers had no option but to return to Murmansk.

How restful and wonderful, after all your hardships, it must have been to sail from Vardo through the fjords* (see footnote opposite) on to Bergen and finally to your grandparents' house in Scotland.

Aunt Nelly's letter, as you would know, was written in English. Sadly, being blind, my uncle could not read it. My father, who knew a little English, was able to make out some parts of it, but it was Ghermosha's godfather, Aleksandr Aleksandrovich, who, sent for post haste, read it over several times and from that day on read and replied to all letters from Aunt Nelly to Uncle Gherman over the years. Perhaps you may still have some of them?

There was this other letter from you Jenya, which I remember, being young at the time, laboriously reading to my uncle. It was written in Russian and had arrived shortly after the one we received from Aunt Nelly. You wrote that Ghermosha and you were now attending school in Broughty Ferry. Ghermosha had quite settled down, was enjoying his lessons and making friends with his school mates. You on the other hand were not happy in the small private school for girls chosen by your grandfather. With the exception of two young sisters who, living nearby, accompanied you to and from school and often invited you to their home, most of the other girls were cold and distant. You missed the old Mariyanskaya Gymnaziya, the girls who shared your school life throughout the many years and especially your close friends, Valya Lazareva and Shura Rubtsova.

The spelling was strange and difficult compared to Russian and poor Aunt Nelly was having quite a time when helping you and Ghermosha with your homework.

The headmistress was a pleasant lady, you wrote, but not so the second in command who had a nasty temper, and when impatient would slap the girls or pull their hair.

You were obviously unhappy but a letter you wrote later had a more cheerful tone. You mentioned that the headmistress had died suddenly, the school was closed down and you were now attending business college where the atmosphere was more relaxed and you were making new friends.

* At this point I have to add that the lovely journey through the Norwegian fjords to which Evgenie refers would never have taken place if it were not for a miraculous incident in a small room of the Custom sheds in Murmansk. Each one of us was taken in turn there and under the watchful eyes of a very strict woman had to undress and have our clothing searched. It so happened that, previous to our departure from Archangel, we were warned that no foreign currency was permitted to be taken out of Russia and any attempted smuggling would be severely punished. This same warning was repeated in the customs shed, prior to us being searched and boarding the trawler.

On the previous evening, in our cabin aboard the *Sever*, we tried to hide a few articles. My mother, who had very little jewellery, sewed inside the pleats of her dress one or two brooches and her diamond engagement ring. On the other hand, our friend Madame Ankirova not only sewed her pearl necklace in a cuff of her blouse, but hid in the soles of her stockings a substantial sum in Norwegian currency. She also possessed a pair of valuable aquamarine earrings styled in the shape of small marbles which my brother and I, against our mother's strong objections, enthusiastically offered to hide inside our mouths.

The shameful search began the following morning. My young brother was taken first. Although he wept loudly when his precious watch – a present from his Scots grandfather – was confiscated he did not betray the earring in his mouth. Nor did I when taken next and I stood shivering while the woman searched through my clothing. My mother followed and there again the brooches inside her dress were not detected. The last one to go in was our friend Mme Ankirova. There likewise she completely undressed and sat down to pull off her stockings. As she did so, the hard expression on the woman's face softened and lifting her hand she suddenly said, 'Just leave your stockings on Matushka [Little Mother].' Madame Ankirova was saved and we along with her.

This incident and many others were never mentioned in any letters to my father or to Evgenie as it would have been courting trouble to do so.

In conclusion I may add that all I have described has been written previously elsewhere but perhaps bears repeating.

Meanwhile, Uncle was glad to learn that your grandparents welcomed your arrival, as did all the Cameron family and that you were happy to be in Scotland where the people were friendly but for some reason liked to talk about the weather. There was no shortage of food and wonderful sweetie shops.

How envious I was when reading about these sweetie shops for I had no memory of ever having tasted a sweet.

What vexed my uncle was you mentioning in your letter that all the roubles* Aunt Nelly brought had proved to be worthless.

These letters from Scotland, and the hope that you might return one day, were, I believe, the sole reasons for my uncle's existence. How he fretted if there was a long interval between them and how overjoyed he was when at last the longed for letter arrived.

Each of your birthdays was a matter of great importance and was solemnly celebrated each year. It was as if he believed he still remained close to you.

All his friends used to gather around him. Aleksandr Aleksandrovich would come along as did the old deacon from the Church of the Assumption – a faithful visitor, who wrote many of my uncle's letters – also Uncle Yura (who, as you perhaps remember, was my godfather), some others and of course my father. There would be a bottle of vodka and a little something to eat with it brought by each guest. Later, after Babushka returned from exile, she would likewise arrive bringing some tasty speciality of her baking.

Then came the moment when everyone lifted their glass. I can still see my uncle sitting up in bed and asking his friends to drink to the health of his wife, son or daughter as the occasion arose.

These birthday celebrations were repeated year after year until his death.

You must not grieve, Jenya, when you read these lines, for as much as your father longed for you all, and I have to admit there were times when I found him sad and silent, he was usually cheerful and never

* Prior to our departure from Archangel my mother was led to believe that although it was known that Russian currency was not accepted abroad there was an exception for notes featuring the head of Alexander III. Poor Mama had run around selling some of her valuable possessions such as her watch and a string of pearls. At the same time we had to think of Father and leave for him such things as a complete dinner and tea set, a samovar and Ghermosha's school uniform, the latter considered to be of great value, all of which he was later able to exchange for food.

After collecting thousands of these special roubles, she packed them in a small cotton bag. On arrival in Vardo she took them to the nearest bank only to be told that these special notes were like the rest of Russian currency – just worthless bits of paper. Bitterly disappointed, she had no option but to send a telegram to my grandfather who immediately sent off the money required to cover the journey to Scotland.

The little cotton bag I may add is still in my possession. It has long since lost its pristine freshness but the notes inside are still as new as on the day my mother hopefully packed them.

47

lonely as every day there were friends who called to see him with whom he joked and held long conversations. Even many of our young friends came to the house. Petya Scroznikov often called as did Tolya Mamontov, the leader of your gang. Your school friend Valya Lazareva came one day. She was eager to have your address as she wished to keep in touch with you. They were all very interested to hear about Scotland and how you settled down there. I knew all your friends and still remember their visits over the years.

Did you know that Petya Scroznikov died during the terrible thirties? Tolya Mamontov became a very important commissar and another of your playmates, Volodya Zaborchikov, the son of the general executed at the start of the revolution, fought through the whole of this last war and survived with the loss of a leg! I do not know what happened to his sister Vera. Having lived now for many years in Leningrad I lost touch with the people in Archangel.

Please convey my thanks to Ronald for the photographs. Your husband, Jenya, takes a good picture, they are very clear and interesting and we enjoyed seeing them, I think, like Victoria, you bear a strong resemblance to our Babushka.

I have begun to arrange all the pictures you send to us in an album. It will be something rather special.

Meanwhile my wife Elena and I wish you good health and happiness. Please write!

Yours,
Evgenie

July 1974

Dear Jenya,

Today I have received a wonderful surprise, when, on opening my post-box, I found not one but two letters from you, for which I thank you very much.

I note you have just returned to Edinburgh from a visit to Michael and his family in the country. I am glad to read that you all enjoyed yourselves in spite of the rainy weather. I was interested to note that Ronald was driving his Citroen car. Here Citroen cars are rarely seen and usually belong to foreigners. As far as the ordinary members of the population such as me are concerned – not many own a car.

Just now Leningrad is basking in warm sunny weather. I am at my desk writing to you with our cat Yashka sitting there as well watching me intently. Elena is busily engaged watering the plants growing in our balcony. It is a sunny little corner where my wife loves to potter with her flowers. The seeds you sent to us have now produced lovely lilac-coloured blossoms with a delightful sweet scent. As we do not know their names we refer to them as 'Strangers'.

We live on the fifth floor in a high-rise building of nine storeys. In our apartment there are three rooms and a kitchen, bathroom, balcony and a corridor with a roomy press and a lift. We are supplied with a fridge, washing machine, cooker, electricity and gas. A great boon is the constant supply of hot and cold water.

This building is situated in the outskirts of the city and is comparatively new. We have been living here only since 1971. Nearby there is still a bit of countryside with trees, wild flowers and a small lake where Elena and I enjoy walking.

Our apartment costs eighteen roubles per month. To that is added fifteen kopecks for gas per each person.

My pension is 110 roubles a month, Elena's eighty roubles. We live comfortably but not extravagantly. Elena is a good plain cook. Sometimes she serves her dishes accompanied by a glass or two of vodka, but such luxuries as expensive wines, caviar and the like are not for us.

Men receive their pensions when they reach sixty years of age and women at fifty-five. The average pension for men, in this year of 1975, is 110 to 120 roubles and for women eighty roubles. There are of course higher figures about which we are not told.

We are always very interested to read about your way of life in Scotland about which we know very little. What amazes us is that you in the United Kingdom still talk about inches, yards, and pounds. We have long since abolished this system and refer instead to metres and kilos.

From what you write I have come to the conclusion that our food on the whole is cheaper than in Scotland except perhaps sugar for which we pay ninety kopecks per kilo. The price of coffee for some strange reason has risen to twenty roubles per kilo, but as our health is not so good, we never touch it and always drink tea instead.

What is far greater than yours is the price we have to pay for our clothing and especially so if it comes from the West.

Elena had to pay 270 roubles for her winter coat of medium quality and a man's suit will cost us from 160 to 200 roubles.

Recently it was very necessary for Elena to acquire new boots. The pair she bought a year ago, manufactured in Russia from artificial leather, cost thirty roubles and were now shabby and useless. Elena was determined to find a pair of good quality boots in real leather, preferably from the West. Unfortunately the price of eighty roubles was more than she could afford, but undaunted she decided to 'look around'. This 'saga of the boots' as I called it, lasted three long weeks. In the end, just as we were despairing of finding anything that would please my wife, luck favoured us with the discovery of an old shoe-maker. He made a handsome pair of high boots from the best quality leather for the modest price of fifty roubles. In my eyes they were a bit too wide at the top, but my darling is happy and quite unaware that she presents a strong resemblance to the mythical character of 'Puss in Boots'.

In reading your second letter I was astonished and frankly envious to learn that when preparing to entertain some friends to a party, you had bought a whole salmon. *A whole salmon!* Such a fish we have not seen for many years and the wonderful 'Dvina salmon' is only a distant memory. Fresh herring has also vanished and cod very rarely appears in the market. Here we are offered a variety of fish brought from warm seas which unfortunately are very inferior to those caught in northern waters. The other week there was a rumour that cod was available in our local market. I immediately rushed out and came back triumphantly carrying four kilos of lovely fresh cod. Delighted with my purchase, we placed one half in the fridge and salted the rest.

These are the little events that bring some colour to our life. On the whole we are content. There is the television, occasional trips to the theatre and visits from our children. It wasn't always so. You can't imagine how difficult was our life in the aftermath of the last war when we were living in a two-roomed flat near the Moscow Station. It was especially hard when our two children were young and Elena and I had to work. Fortunately the children did well at school. Our daughter Natasha was a talented child, often chosen to take part in plays. After completing ten years of her education she joined the Rimsky-Korsakov School of Music where she was taught how to present herself on the stage. Natasha is not a singer as such but an entertainer, she plays the guitar, dances, acts and sings a little. She is attached to the Leningrad TV and is a member of a group who not only appear on the television but travel all over Russia. She has also been in East Germany, Poland, Czechoslovakia and Bulgaria. Her dream is to travel farther abroad to see France, Britain etc. but the group is not allowed to perform in capitalist countries.

Our son Sergei has also done well for himself and is a qualified television engineer as is his young wife whom he recently married. They were trained in the same Institute. We are happy when they visit us occasionally, but of course, like most young people they lead their own lives.

What I have described, dear Jenya, is a picture of my life in Leningrad where I have now spent thirty years. In my next letter I should like to tell you about the distant events and the way of life during your absence.

Meantime I embrace and kiss you. Elena sends her warm regards to you and Ronald,

With best wishes

Evgenie

August 1974

Dear Jenya,

Yesterday I received your welcome letter. It appears to have been a long time flying and arrived torn at one end and stuck together by adhesive tape. Someone somewhere I suspect has been inordinately curious, but at least was kind enough to let me have my letter!

Here autumn has arrived, the days are growing shorter and at times a cold wind blows from the Gulf of Finland. I understand that Edinburgh is likewise windy – the climate of the two cities seems to be alike.

You may be surprised to learn that at one time my father toyed with the idea of leaving Russia and settling in Scotland or some other part in the West. As you know, my father, having invested his inheritance in some gold mines in Siberia and deriving a good income out of his shares, never worked at all, enjoying instead a life of leisure in a separate flat in Babushka's house. After some disagreement, he moved to the house in Uspenskaya Ulitza and married my mother.

In early 1919, following the revolution, many people left Archangel, including our relatives, and having transferred their money first to Britain, then later to Germany, led a comfortable existence there. My father thought of following their example but in the end decided against it. He had been in Scotland on a short holiday and liked the country and the Scots very much, but simply could not see himself living anywhere else but in Russia. He did not realise at the time that in the end all his investments would be lost and there would be no income to support himself and his family. In this desperate situation Father tried to find work but all his applications were refused for the simple reason that he was a member of a well-known family who at one time were wealthy owners of timber mills and therefore classed as enemies of the people. He was eventually sent to a logging camp to assist in rolling the logs down to the river. Never having performed any physical labour in his life he only succeeded in straining his back and was dismissed. From then on he was unable to find work of any description.

At times when looking back on these difficult early twenties I am reminded that the worst feature of our existence was the terrible problem with water and fuel. As you will remember, Jenya, very few houses had water laid on and even the best of them had to rely on its being brought to the house.

In those far-off days there was a group of men who ran a profitable business delivering water to the various houses. It was a common sight to see them passing along the streets driving their horse-drawn carts or sledges in winter laden with the huge barrels. This enterprise, so helpful to the inhabitants, was later regarded as a capitalist venture and abolished by the authorities. To us such a situation was disastrous. I, ten years old at the time, was the eldest in the family and as my father was unable to be of any assistance the work of supplying the house with water fell upon my shoulders. For one so young it was a Herculean task and especially so in the dead of winter. In the adjoining street known as the Sadovaya Ulitza, stood a kiosk from which water could be obtained in return for a token. It was my custom each day to set off for Sadovaya Ulitza with my sledge and two buckets and again repeat this journey as that quantity of water was never sufficient for a family such as ours. These journeys were hard going at the best of times, but made more hazardous by the gang wars between the boys in Sadovaya Ulitza and those who lived in our Uspenskaya Ulitza, later renamed Proletarskaya. All too often, after having filled my buckets and wending my way home, I would suddenly be attacked by members of the opposing gang, determined to empty my buckets on to the snow.

I fought bitterly to defend my precious cargo, at times helped by a friendly passer-by or the boys from our own street, but all too often would arrive home with a bleeding nose or a bump on the head.

Harrowing also were the expeditions to the river for the rinsing of the clothes and sheets in the water holes. I usually helped my mother and can still remember seeing her weeping while ringing out the ice-cold washing. On one such occasion we were suddenly caught up in a blinding snowstorm and only after a frightening struggle to reach the shore, eventually succeeded in arriving at the house in the last stages of exhaustion.

Even yet after a lapse of many years as I am sitting writing this letter, I ask myself how did we succeed in surviving such terrible hardships?

Another source of anxiety, was the problem of how to keep the house warm during the extreme cold of our severe winters. The fuel was timber cut into suitable lengths and formed into a stack measuring 216 cubic feet. It was known as a 'Sajen' and sold as such at an exorbitant price. Many people unable to find the money were forced to burn old fences, sheds, wooden pavements and so on.

My mother, blessed with clever hands, was able to earn some money by sewing. Unfortunately as there were no longer any shops selling material, her clients brought old coats, suits, dresses etc to be remade into suitable garments. Uncle Gherman was actually better off than we were, as on top of a pension from the government he received parcels and money from his cousins in Germany. Aunt Nelly likewise sent parcels and in every letter from Scotland were enclosed Gillette blades, a very precious commodity, much in demand, enabling him to exchange them for food.

Our greatest benefactor was Aunt Olga in Finland. She was our Guardian Angel sending us parcels and money. Without her assistance we would have been in a very bad way. Yet in spite of all the help life was becoming more difficult. We were forced to exchange for food or sell our belongings and finally were left with empty rooms with the exception of beds and a few chairs. I remember how sad we children were watching our piano being removed in exchange for forty kilos of potatoes.

At the same time I cannot say, Jenya, that we children ever thought we were miserable. It was a way of life that went on and not all was gloom.

In our street, quite near our house, stood the town *banya* [bath house] named Uspenskaya and from what I have heard is still functioning after all these long years. There we adjourned every week, revelling in the abundance of warm water, filling tubs and basins, emptying them over each other, frolicking in the steamy heat and arriving home scrubbed and refreshed.

The summers, too, were always joyful. We swam and fished in the river, gathered mushrooms and berries in the woods and played games in the street.

Jenya, I have been writing all morning but have not answered some of your questions. They will be dealt with during the next week. Meanwhile I will post this from the Main Post Office which is situated near St Isaac's Cathedral and quite a long way from our house. I am enclosing some pictures which may interest you.

Our regards to Ronald and the boys. I kiss and embrace you,

Evgenie

October 1974

Dear Jenya,

I am so sorry I am late in writing my promised letter, but recently I have had to attend the eye clinic where I am receiving treatment for something that at times accompanies old age which they warn me could lead to total blindness – a calamity I trust I will not live to endure.

Meanwhile to our joy a second letter has arrived from you, but has once again been opened and stuck together. We wonder if perhaps the post-woman may have put it in the wrong box! Your letters to us are always very interesting. We read them over and over again. The snaps, taken in India, which you enclosed are also of great interest, not only to me and Elena, but to all the members of the family. How strange has been your fate to be born and bred in Arctic regions and to spend so much of your married life in tropical India and Thailand. How I envy you and how different has been my life.

You are asking me in your letter if I knew when Babushka and Dedushka returned from exile. As far as I can recall, I believe it was in the summer of 1923. Doctors and surgeons were very scarce at that time in Archangel. They settled at first with Marga and Dmitry and their children, Volodya and Liza, but later moved to another house which stood on the corner of Pomorskaya Ulitza and the main street, the name of which was changed from Troitsky Prospect to Ulitza Pavlina Vinogradova. It was a large house which at one time belonged to the wealthy merchant, Sabinin, who had vanished, like many more. In the house lived various families and our grandparents were allotted two spacious rooms. The pieces of furniture and articles saved from the fire, including Dedushka's writing desk, were arranged in these rooms where he continued treating various patients. They flocked to him in the evenings after he returned from the hospital in which he had resumed his previous post as a surgeon.

All the other tenants in the house were educated, pleasant people who got on well with Babushka and Dedushka.

The exception was a woman – a Tatar or Chechenka – who had the fear of death on all the other tenants and when preparing her food demanded that she would be the sole occupant of the kitchen. Any intruder was threatened with a long-handled poker and chased out.

Following complaints from the indignant tenants a policeman arrived on the scene and she chased him out too. He never returned and this dreadful woman continued to lord it over the helpless occupiers.

Babushka never again saw her house or garden and never went near the street. To us she brought great joy and comfort, keeping the family together, visiting us and helping in every way she could.

Another joyful event was the arrival of Kapochka from Leningrad who used to be the housekeeper in Babushka's house and was very close to you, Jenya, and taught you all our old Russian songs. Kapochka stayed with us, helped my mother with the sewing and ironing and to my uncle's great joy took over the caring of him from the useless and lazy woman he had employed previously. I still remember seeing Kapochka ironing away and singing in full voice while we children sat enthralled listening and sometimes joining in.

Ten years later I had occasion to visit Leningrad where I knew Kapochka was living, having left Archangel. After some searching I found her. She was staying with her sister in a small single room, the window of which looked out on to a high dark wall. There was hardly any furniture in that room but she welcomed me warmly, hurried to put on the samovar and the three of us sat talking well into the night. After the end of the Second World War in 1946, I was back again in Leningrad. There was no trace of the house or of Kapochka and her sister. They had perished during the historic siege of Leningrad.

Just now as I write these lines Natasha has called. She had been with her group performing in Helsinki and while there dropped a note to Leo, the son of my late cousin Marina whose address she knew. She regretted she was not allowed to pay any calls but thought she would like to convey her regards to him. Natasha has traversed the whole of Russia performing in all the towns but feels frustrated as the group is not permitted to visit such countries as Scotland where she might have had the chance to meet you.

There is a lot I should like to tell you about these distant days and hope to continue as time goes on, but meanwhile I wish you and yours all the best in the present and future. I kiss and embrace you and look forward to receiving your next letter.

Evgenie

February 1975

Dear Jenya,

Today we have been gladdened by the arrival of your long-awaited letter and note that you have had a busy time with some old friends from India staying with you.

Here nothing unusual has been happening. We are alive and comparatively well. Elena still continues working. The office where she is employed as the cashier is situated quite near us, but I make a point of meeting her at the end of the working day as at present in the gathering darkness it is possible for some hooligan to attack and rob a pedestrian.

We have been studying again the photos of you and Ronald with your boys taken in India during the war years and are fascinated by the picture of the twins standing with their Indian nurse beside these tropical palms.

Always when I begin to write to you my thoughts go back to scenes of long ago. It is as if I am reliving my life. What springs to mind is the long-awaited arrival of our Aunt Olga from Finland in the early summer of 1924. It was a very joyful event and a happy reunion between our fathers and their beloved sister whom they had not seen for eight long years. Our generous aunt brought numerous gifts forgetting no one. As well as clothing there were toys and sweets for us children – something we had not seen for a very long time. She spent many hours sitting beside Uncle Gherman reminiscing about their early years. She stayed with Babushka but sadly her visit was all too short and at the end of a mere two weeks she had to return to Finland. I remember seeing her and my uncle weeping as they clung to each other. Both knew they would never meet again.

When leaving Aunt Olga took back with her a few ikons, which, following the abolition of religion during that period, were no longer considered to be of any value. The large ikon of St Nicholas, which had been in the family for generations and was reputed to be miraculous, was likewise carefully packed and accompanied our aunt to Finland. My parents had succeeded in dragging it out when Babushka's house was on fire, but as we had no recollections of any miracles performed on our behalf, there were no regrets when parting from it. Later our Aunt wrote saying that everything had arrived safely in Helsinki.*

We missed Aunt Olga very much and kept hoping that she would return but we never saw her again.

Meanwhile, during that year of 1924 many changes were taking place in the town. Do you remember, Jenya, the piers that jutted out over the water at the end of the streets leading down to the river? I am

---

* What Evgenie never discovered, and I only years later through my late aunt's granddaughters, was that after Aunt Olga's death the ikon of St Nicholas was passed on to her only son, Igor, who in turn bequeathed it to the Russian Orthodox Cathedral in Helsinki where it remains to this day.

reminded of the one at the foot of Olonetskaya Street where stood our Babushka's house. What a lively place it was during the hot summer days. Peasants crossed over from the islands with their cargoes of butter, milk and eggs. Women gossiped together while rinsing their clothes. Old men and little boys, their legs dangling over the side, sat fishing. In short, the pier was a hive of activity which lasted until the late autumn when, prior to the river freezing, all the piers were removed and the timbers piled neatly at the side of the roads. In the spring when the last of the ice floes sailed away to the White Sea the piers were rebuilt and the people gathered there once again just as they did year after year. In the end the authorities did away with these structures and instead there is now a wide expanse of golden sands with men and women lazing in the sun and the children playing nearby.

The wooden bridge carrying all the traffic, including the tramways between Archangel and the island of Solombala, was likewise dismantled in the autumn, but soon after, when the river had frozen to the required depth, the tram lines were relaid directly on the ice and all links were resumed until the spring when the whole process was repeated in reverse.

Each spring there was a period, lasting a few days, when the headlong rush of the breaking ice cut off all contacts between the town and Solombala, causing great inconvenience to the people on both sides of the river.

Some time in 1924 our local government decided to build a new bridge, one which would stand up against the extreme pressure of the ice. It was strongly constructed – high enough to allow ships to sail under and wide enough for double tramway lines plus all the traffic between the two shores.

In the summer of 1925 occurred the opening of the bridge, attended by important members of the main government. There were speeches, music, singing and a great feeling of jubilation among the crowd attending this rare occasion.

The bridge stood firmly all summer and winter, but when spring arrived and the ice began to break up, onlookers gathered and stood watching with bated breath. At first the ice flowed gently under the bridge but gradually the speed and force increased. The bridge resisted, strongly defending itself, but all too soon was heard the frightening roar of the cracking beams. The tramway lines were thrown up like ribbons, the centre of the bridge collapsed and together with the ice, was carried out to sea.

To the horrified onlookers this awesome scene brought grief and disappointment. For several years following that disaster the people crossed to Solombala on a pontoon bridge, but in 1954 a strong bridge suspended on steel cables was erected which proved capable of withstanding the strongest pressure of the ice and is still there as I write these lines.

This has been a rather long letter but before I finish I should like you to thank Ghermosha on my behalf for his kind regards to me. I fully understand why he has forgotten how to write in Russian. He is younger than you and having spent so many years in Venezuela where they speak Spanish it is not surprising that the language of his childhood left him. Thank God that the same fate did not overtake you! Your letters are a great source of interest to us for which I am very grateful. Please continue writing.

We all send our best wishes to Ghermosha and all the members of the family.

I kiss and embrace you.

Evgenie.

P.S. How is Ron? You say very little about him.

————————————

January 1976

Dear Jenya,

Today at long last I received your welcome letter with the beautiful Christmas card which we shall cherish and will place in a special album where I keep all your cards and pictures. We were beginning to wonder if all was well with you, but note by the post-mark that your letter has been on the road for twenty days. There is no accounting for such a strange delay.

You tell me that you have been trying to create some order out of the great mass of letters collected through the years and have noticed amongst them a bundle of very carefully written letters in pencil – now almost faded – which you believe were written by me. You are correct Jenya, as, when I was almost ten years old, I became your father's chief writer! 'Jenchick, my boy,' he used to say, 'get your pencil and paper and I'll dictate you a letter!'

Of course, I must add that at the end of my writing I was usually rewarded by an interesting story. My uncle was a gifted teller of tales.

In the early days of his youth he had travelled to many parts of the world, sailed over tropical seas and oceans and watched the flying fish leap out of the waves as dolphins danced alongside the ship. He had admired the splendour of the Taj Mahal in India, the Golden Temples of Siam and Burma and been involved in no end of strange adventures.

I listened spellbound to Uncle's wondrous accounts of his travels to these distant lands so far removed from my own prosaic world.

At times we were joined by my three-year-old sister Olga. She would sit with her doll at Uncle Gherman's feet, watch our faces intently with her serious eyes, smile when we laughed and though not understanding what it was all about was happy to be with us.

One of my uncle's most amazing adventures occurred when he was travelling on an old sailing ship from Singapore to India. There were only a few passengers aboard, including a young Malaysian girl.

Somewhere in the Indian Ocean fire broke out and spread like lightning, leaving no option but for the crew and passengers to abandon the ship and take to a lifeboat, but no sooner had they cast off than the young Malaysian girl appeared on deck. They had forgotten all about her! Undaunted, the girl leapt from the ship and with her full skirt spreading out like a parachute, she landed on the water, light as a bird.

For two days they suffered heat, thirst and hunger until to their great relief they saw on the horizon the green line of a small island. On arrival they were met by some friendly natives and spent a few days in this small paradise where there was an abundance of fish, coconuts and bananas. A passing ship picked them up and took them on to India from where my uncle eventually arrived safely in Europe.

I loved that story – especially the parts describing coconuts and bananas which I had never seen, far less tasted.

Of course, as I grew older I realised that all my uncle's amazing accounts of his travels were only the creation of a rich imagination. He had never seen any golden temples, tropical islands and certainly no girl with the full skirt on which she came down as if on a parachute. It was all out of his head and although he had travelled extensively, he had actually never been out of Europe.

What, however, Uncle Gherman never realised was that by relating these enchanting stories, he instilled in me a burning desire to reach those same magic shores. 'Yes,' I promised myself, 'I will also see the flying fish and dancing dolphins.'

I was determined to work hard at school to gain admittance to our Sea College. From there, after obtaining the necessary qualification, I hoped to join a ship sailing to those distant shores. Such were the dreams of a ten-year-old boy. I kept them close to my heart revealing nothing to anyone. I am inclined to be carried away by my memories of the past to the exclusion of the present. I hope you won't find them too tedious.

We are now moving into another year. Elena and I as usual prepared our New Year table with the hope that the children might join us. We were not disappointed. They all arrived and we spent a very happy evening together. They were very interested to read your letter and talked a lot about you. When twelve o'clock struck we all drank to the health of you and your family in the coming year.

Jenya, how wonderful it would be if there was a magic carpet which could have brought you here to celebrate this year together.

I embrace and kiss you. Write! Write!

Evgenie

April 1976

Dear Jenya,

I am sitting alone in the house. Elena has gone to her office and there is only Yashka the cat for company. The rain is beating against the windows. It is rather lonesome.

Your later letter of a fortnight ago I have answered but feel I should like to continue.

Here Easter has come and gone almost unnoticed. Our children having never been taught religion are not religious and know nothing about it. Elena occasionally attends the church. Her mother, who perished during the siege of Leningrad, was a very faithful adherent and something must have rubbed off from her on to Elena.

As for me, having been born at the start of the world war in 1914 and experienced the gradual decline in the way of life in the years which followed, there is no memory of the great Easter festivities such as related to me by our babushka. I do remember, however, one small celebration which took place in 1926 when Uncle Seryozha with his wife and little son, Yurie, arrived from Leningrad to spend a holiday with Babushka.

They came to our house on Easter Sunday. Babushka brought a few coloured eggs, the traditional 'Kulich' [a special cake] and 'Pascha' [a conical shaped cheese prepared from cottage cheese, sugar, and whipped cream]. Everything was placed on a table beside Uncle Gherman and we all gathered round him. Little Yurie aged two climbed up on the bed beside Uncle and sat there chattering to him in his own style which amused and delighted us all. Little did we think that this same child who became a brilliant student would die from starvation during the siege of Leningrad.

The year 1926 stands out in my memory. Our life was becoming increasingly difficult. Although it was possible to buy more food we had no money to do so. Certain restrictions on trading were lifted, but a new order came out forbidding the acceptance of parcels from friends abroad. This was a severe blow to us all and a source of frustration to our relatives abroad. Aunt Nelly wrote saying that a parcel she sent to Uncle Gherman containing such items as sugar, tea, sardines, jam and a jar of pickles in mustard which Uncle Gherman had requested was returned to her with all the contents broken and mixed up and only fit to be thrown out. However, she still continued to enclose Gillette blades in her letters and our relatives in Germany and Aunt Olga in Finland were not debarred from sending money which helped us to survive.

My father, unfortunately, due to his family name and writing letters to his sister in Finland, was unable in spite of all his efforts to obtain work of any kind. This caused a great deal of friction between him and my mother who likewise was not receiving the same sewing orders for the simple reason that there was no more clothing to alter or cloth to buy. Everything saleable in the house was sold and Uncle Gherman had to part with his beautiful dinner set which he had cherished over the years.

Yet during these dark times there occurred an event which brightened our days for a little while, days I recall with some amusement tinged with sadness.

It so happened that in spite of the restrictions a small parcel arrived one day for Uncle Gherman. On opening this box we discovered a strange little machine accompanied by instructions printed in English. After a great deal of conjecture my father was able to discover that this was a gadget for sharpening razor blades.

On hearing this my Uncle in some excitement turned to me. 'Jenchik,' he said, 'go up to the garret where you will find a roll of wall-paper.' This I was instructed to cut up in pieces and print on them in large letters SAFETY RAZOR BLADES CAN BE SHARPENED HERE. The address which followed was printed in small letters and no price was mentioned to avoid any suggestion of capitalism.

During the years of want, men found it impossible to purchase razor blades and therefore various means were used for shaving, at times with disastrous results.

Soon after displaying our posters at various strategic points, customers started to arrive with their rusty blades. My uncle and I decided that the method of sharpening them would be shared between us. I would slip the blade into the slot on the machine and he would turn the little handle. The instructions were for the handle to be turned twenty times, which we followed in the beginning but soon reduced the number to ten!

The response was far greater than we expected and payment being made in kind, for some time it could be said we were living it up! Men lined up bringing sugar, butter, flour and occasionally meat and game, but the greatest reward of all was in the shape of a large handsome cock with magnificent plumage in black, gold and crimson. He was a proud bird. Holding high his fiery red crest, he strutted up and down the room, claws tapping the wooden floor, occasionally casting a contemptuous glance in our direction. We ate every bit of him.

Leaving only his beak and claws, we feasted for two days, relishing each morsel of this delectable gift from the gods. Sadly, all too soon came retribution. Our customers returned, loudly protesting that the blades very quickly became quite useless and threatened to report us if we did not return whatever they had given. This was of course impossible. The sugar and butter was used up, the money spent and the cock eaten. The threats alarmed us. The only way out was to re-sharpen the blades free of charge.

Well I remember how my uncle and I laboured to placate our customers sometimes well into the White Arctic nights. Our hands became cut and bleeding; we were exhausted, but still continued until one day the wretched machine suddenly disintegrated. My uncle sighed deeply with relief. 'Our business is finished,' he remarked, 'we'll have to think of something else.' Sadly the 'something else' never materialised. Our struggle for existence went on.

At times we were helped by Babushka who, when calling, would bring a few eggs, a bit of fish or whatever. She was in a better position than us as Dedushka often received payments in kind from his patients. There were also occasions when Uncle Yura invited me to accompany him on a shooting expedition. I loved those outings and would jubilantly return carrying a rabbit or a bird of some kind, but these events occurred very rarely as Uncle Yura was tied up in his work and often away from home.

In 1926 my mother decided to send my sister Victoria to St Petersburg to stay with our cousin Irina, the daughter of Aunt Olga. Irina was married to Baron Peter Brok who was a colonel in the famous Semyonovski Regiment – now disbanded. Miraculously, Peter along with a few fellow officers escaped execution and was now living at peace with his young wife and their little girl, likewise named Irina.

My sister Victoria, better known as Vika, was blessed with a very cheerful disposition and although only ten years old set off undaunted on the long monotonous train journey of two days to Leningrad where she was met by Irina and Peter and settled down with them for the next few years. Later, as she grew older, she learned to drive a car and in the same undaunted style used to drive important commissars to and from their work. Vika married a communist and as I write these lines they still live happily together with their children.

In the summer of 1927, with no improvement in our lifestyle and my parents drifting apart, my mother decided to leave our dear Archangel and settle in Kem, a small town on the west shore of the White Sea. There it was said living conditions were better and an old friend offered us accommodation. It was decided that Mother, my brother Shurick, little Olga and I would travel by ship. I was most unhappy but had no option. I remember how on the morning of our departure I said 'Goodbye' to my uncle. He had been saddened by this new arrangement but remained silent. Now he drew his hand over my head and face and quietly said, 'Do not forget me Jenchik. Write to me.' Little did I know that I would never see him again!

I must close on this sad note.

I kiss and embrace you.

Evgenie

November 1977

The town of Kem [Evgenie wrote in his subsequent letter] is a dreary place and cannot be compared with Archangel. I missed my town, our relatives and friends, the boys I played with, but gradually settled down to a different way of life. We shared the house with my mother's friend called Aunty Tanya, who was very kind to us children. Mother soon established herself as a fine dressmaker and attracted numerous customers which helped us to survive.

We heard very little from Archangel but during Christmas of 1927 we received from Babushka a parcel of her home baking. This was followed by another letter from her at the end of January informing us that Uncle Gherman had died on the 13th of that month. I remember how upset I was when reading this tragic news. I had been very attached to my uncle who actually meant more to me than my own father.

In her letter Babushka wrote that after we left, towards the end of the year Uncle's condition deteriorated and he appeared to have lost interest in everything. The family had gathered round him and she herself remained constantly by his side, staying overnight to keep him company. Towards the end he imagined that Aunt Nelly had decided to return with the children just as she did in 1919 and with that happy thought peacefully slipped away.

On the third day after his death, according to our custom, he was taken to the Church of the Assumption, to remain there overnight. The following day the funeral service was held by Father Dmitry who had known all our family since we were born. He was joined by the Archimandrite from the Cathedral who at the end of the service gave a moving speech. The church was packed with people holding lighted candles. It was just like Easter.

'Outside it was bitterly cold,' Babushka went on, 'but your father and I walked with the other mourners to the cemetery. Your uncle was buried quite near his own father, your grandfather Aleksandr Scholts who, by a strange coincidence, had also died on 13 January (in 1890) – the day of Uncle's ninth birthday.'

Such was the sad account by Babushka of Uncle Gherman's death. I trust, Jenya, you will not be too upset by it.

Meanwhile our life in Kem was not proving to be any easier than in Archangel. Our mother worked hard sewing dresses, at times well into the night, but there was never enough money to feed us.

In early spring I reached my fourteenth birthday and, having finished eight classes at school, decided to look for work. My ambition was still to go to sea and find a place on some ship, but no matter how hard I searched, running round all the shipping offices and wharves, there were only refusals. I realised that, like my father in Archangel, my name and distant background was against me. We were now into early summer. Time was flying, the wharfs were busy. Becoming more despondent with each passing day, I watched with envy the coming and going of all the ships.

One morning my mother met by chance an old friend who happened to be the skipper of a sail-driven trawler. On hearing about my difficulties he kindly told her to send me along to his ship the next day and he would look me over. The ship, named *The Red Hunter*, was preparing to leave for Murmansk.

The following morning, Mother rolled up a clean shirt round a thick slice of black bread and together we went down to the wharf. There she kissed and blessed me, gave a few words of advice, handed over the parcel, and hurriedly left to get on with her work.

It was a beautiful morning with the sun gliding slowly on the horizon – not a soul to be seen with only the sharp cry of the gulls breaking the silence.

My beloved cousin, Evgenie, whose letters told me so much
about life in Russia after we left. This photograph was taken
in 1985 shortly before his death.

Babushka and Uncle Sanya beside my father's grave.

The little church beside the cemetery where my father and other members of the family are buried.

The House by the Dvina as it was . . . . now all gone.

Here were the gates . . . .

With Yuri in our old garden.

The beautiful cathedral in Archangel as it was in 1917.
It was later completely destroyed.

The drama school built on the site of the cathedral.

Archangel as it was . . .

. . . and as it is now.

My cousin Yura's son Alexei photographed as an officer
in the Russian Air Force.

In the garden of our house with my cousin Olga *(right)*
when she stayed with us in 1987.

Two views of my beloved Dvina. When I was a child the beach was completely different with boulders and wild plants growing there.

The Red Hunter was standing at the end of the pier. I settled down on a coil of rope and prepared to wait, but kept glancing at the ship, alternating between hope and despair. The hours passed slowly. Although not hungry I ate the bread and shortly after a group of men came along to the ship. On timidly approaching them, I found my skinny form being appraised in a sceptical manner. 'Let's see you climb to the top of that mast,' ordered one of them. There was no time to hesitate. I jumped up and, climbing as fast as I could, reached the top, where, on looking down, I was horrified to find myself at such a height. Down below my new friends were encouragingly waving their arms. I slid down and stood trembling not knowing whether from fear or joy while they slapped my shoulders and called me 'Molodets' [a brave lad]. I realised I was accepted and the arrival of the skipper confirmed my belief. I was now a full member of the crew.

Soon the sails were raised. *The Red Hunter* slowly began to move away from the pier. I remember standing watching the receding shores as we sailed down the river and into the great expanse of the White Sea. I remember hearing the cry of the gulls, feeling the wind in my face and being overwhelmed by happiness such as I had never known before and would never know again.

My first duty aboard the ship was to prepare the meals for the crew. I had no knowledge of cooking but after the initial blunders, developed an expertise, especially in the preparation of 'ukha' [fish soup] with the main ingredient close at hand straight from the sea. Amongst the other numerous tasks was the cleaning of the galley and the crew's quarters. I worked hard, tried to please and got along well with all the members of the crew and was happy to be one of the boys.

The Red Hunter continued sailing until well into the autumn when, with the approaching freeze up in the North, she was laid up in Kem and I went to live in Archangel with Babushka.

You have asked me, Jenya, to continue describing the events which took place after your departure and the death of your father and Babushka; I shall do so to the best of my ability.

Through you on the other hand I have discovered so much about our distant past of which I knew nothing at all and which has proved to be of absorbing interest, not only to me but to my family also.

More reminiscences in my next letter. Our regards to Ronald.

Yours as always,

Evgenie.

January 1977

Dear Jenya,

I have been looking inside our post-box for the past two weeks but today to my joy recognised the familiar envelope.

I note you have been away staying with Michael and his family in Bristol which I see is in England and quite a bit from Scotland. Michael's house and garden sound very lovely. I did not know that he was such an ardent gardener. This must run in the family as we are also very fond of our little garden on the balcony especially the small lemon tree which blossoms every year but gives no fruit.

We are expecting Vika and her husband tonight and they will be very interested to hear your latest news. Meanwhile I shall devote myself to continuing where I left off in my last letter.

By the end of the summer, although happy being at sea, I came to realise that without additional training in the Sea School, I would never be anything more than a deck hand. I also knew only too well that it would be very difficult to be admitted to the school, but to my great relief through the influence of one of Dedushka's patients a place was found for me in the Archangel Sea College.

Meanwhile, Mother, not happy in Kem, returned to Archangel with Shurick and Olga. Some time earlier, when she was not getting along with my father, she met a man called Victor who had been an officer in the White Army but after being defeated by the Red Army was still living in Archangel. He was now sentenced to serve a term of four years in one of the prison camps in Siberia. My mother, after renewing her acquaintanceship with him on her return from Kem, decided to accompany him. There was still the problem with the two younger children which she solved by taking young Olga with her and leaving Shurick with a friend.

The camp, I learned years later from my mother, was not as bad as some of the others. Situated close to one of the numerous rivers in Siberia, with the great, wild 'Taiga' behind them, they were completely isolated. The work was hard and from what I gathered consisted of the sawing down of trees and the forming of rafts to be sent down the river. The Taiga abounded with a great variety of game and animals, some of which were presented like pets to my little sister who was the only child in the camp. Most of the prisoners were educated men and according to my mother, Victor himself continued with Olga's education.

Four years later, they returned to Archangel from Siberia, walking all the way dragging a sledge with little Olga sitting on top of their few belongings. After spending some time in Archangel, they went on by train to the Ukraine where Victor's mother lived in a small village. There my mother, now married to Victor, settled down with their small daughter, Nora, and my sister Olga.

At times when I look back on those turbulent years when all the members of my family were scattered like autumn leaves by the wind of heaven here and there, I realise how fortunate I was to have lived with my grandparents. For me our Babushka was the most important being in my life and far dearer than our parents. She was at all times kind and attentive, not only to me but to other people as well who often called to ask for advice or help, and yet at the same time courageously and calmly bore her sorrows and misfortunes of which sadly she had so many.

We shared the two rooms already described in my previous letter. My father and I slept in the hall where Dedushka also received his patients. Father, however, was seldom at home and often away for days at a time, engaged on some ploy of his own and it was my duty to collect our rations consisting of bread, sugar, grains and a little butter on which, with the few extras from Dedushka's patients, we managed to exist. Our life was uneventful. We usually gathered in my grandparents' room, where stood a round table, a bookcase, their bed, a few small pieces of furniture along with pictures and an ikon, all retrieved from their house during the fire.

Usually when free in the evening, Dedushka liked to settle down with a book, and Babushka, tired out with her daily chores, also relaxed by reading a passage or two out of the New Testament. Later, she might turn to her favourite hobby of creating beautiful artificial flowers from special materials sent by Aunt Olga from Finland. Babushka was a talented artist in that field and the exquisite life-like flowers she presented to her friends were much treasured by them.

I well remember those wintry nights and can still see the three of us sitting round the table – Dedushka reading, Babushka with her flowers and me poring over my books.

At times Uncle Yura called with his little son, Alexei, or Aunt Marga arrived with her three children – Volodya aged nine, Liza aged seven, and Kolya, just a baby. Marga always spoke in German as she was very afraid the Chechenka woman, who was such a menace, might be listening to the conversation. Marga was also scared to say or do anything that might displease the authorities, as at the back of her mind there was the fear that they might discover that at one time her husband, Dmitry, was in the White Guards and fought against the Red Army.

67

I recollect another occasion when Marga called with Liza. It happened to be near Christmas which, since the abolition of religion, was not celebrated in the same style as previously as the much-loved Christmas trees were forbidden. Both were upset and Liza had obviously been weeping.

It transpired that someone of importance with an original turn of mind had decided to create something in the way of a final gesture to the Christmas tree. Each pupil was told to bring a small Christmas tree and to meet outside the school, where a procession was formed which set off along the main street on to the Cathedral Square. There the trees were thrown down to form a gigantic funeral pyre and set alight. No one expected such a horrifying result. The flames fanned by the wind reached up to the sky, scattering the burning branches far and wide over the square. The children, miraculously unscathed but terrified out of their wits, ran in all directions. Liza in her panic had followed the others and never stopped running until she reached the outskirts of the town, where, cold and exhausted, she was found by her father and brought safely home.

Just now as I describe the incident of so many years ago I have to add that the Christmas tree is back once more in all its glory. There is no religious significance attached to it, but here in Leningrad some parents like to have it and decorate it for their children. Each New Year 'Santa Claus' is likewise welcome, now better known as 'Dedushka Moroz' [Grandpa Frost].

Always when I am writing to you, Jenya, so many scenes and events keep coming back to me which may be new to you.

In the year 1929 Uncle Seryozha arrived with his wife, Masha, and young Yura who, as on the previous occasion, entertained us with his droll remarks so wise beyond his years. We had a happy reunion with all the members of the family in which my father joined in as well. During the conversation it was mentioned there had been a rumour floating around that the government had decided to bring down the cathedral – the pride and glory of the town.

Seryozha, wishing to take a picture, asked me to accompany him to the square. There we duly arrived and to our surprise found a great mass of people had collected, some of whom informed us that this was actually the day chosen for the destruction of the cathedral.

Sure enough, after a little while a group of men arrived on the scene and vanished inside the cathedral. The crowd became silent, no one spoke and as they waited a frightening explosion rent the air demolishing the star-studded cupolas and the magnificent frescoes depicting biblical scenes – reducing everything to a large heap of rubble in a matter of seconds.

Men removed their hats and crossed themselves, women wept and some went down on their knees.

This was the start of the wholesale destruction of every church up and down the river. The Church of the Assumption, attended by our family for generations and where Uncle Gherman was taken prior to his burial, was likewise destroyed with the others. Only one small church was left standing beside the cemetery where funerals and occasional marriage services took place.

Uncle Seryozha, who had taken the picture of the cathedral prior to its destruction, was outraged by this senseless vandalism. He had a great appreciation of art and was an expert in that field.

'Archangel has lost the greatest heritage it ever had – there will never be another one like it,' he exclaimed bitterly as we were wending our way home. He was right. Some time later a drama school replaced the cathedral. A typical modern creation, it had little visual appeal.

Two weeks later Seryozha and his family left for Leningrad and we resumed our usual way of life. I studied hard throughout the long winter nights and was rewarded by high marks in the spring. During the summer I worked anywhere I could. At times on a trawler fishing in the White Sea, or on one of the beautiful paddle steamers, sailing for days on end up the river, halting in villages and small towns. Work was also found in the height of the summer when the great mass of timber rafts began to travel down towards the sawmills where on arrival the beams were delivered on a conveyor system straight from the water to the circular saws. All the mills at one time belonged to individual owners, including my grandfather, something I never dared to mention, but were now in the hands of the government. I worked right on until the start of my studies in the Sea College and the money I earned paid for my keep. Such was my life with which I was content.

It is time to stop and tear myself away from Archangel. Elena sends you her regards and best wishes for a long life and the best of health.

I embrace and kiss you,
Evgenie

───────

October 1977

Dear Jenya,

This morning you have again gladdened my heart by the arrival of your long awaited letter. I note it was posted on the 1st October and

69

has taken exactly three weeks to arrive. The times appear to vary considerably but as long as they do arrive I do not mind.

Inside we found two vanilla sticks and a little packet of cardamom much appreciated by Elena, as such items are not available here. She is also pleased to have the recipe for the dessert 'Pavlova'. It sounds delicious and we are intrigued by the name. You tell me you have large stores in Edinburgh where a great variety of food and clothes can be bought. We also have them. You can take a basket and pick up what you fancy – only we do not always find what we want. At the same time it has to be said that things are slowly improving in our parts. When we first arrived there were only fields and marshes. Now there are roads, gardens, stores and numerous high-rise buildings which although convenient remind me of cardboard boxes.

I am glad you have received the photographs. Although no father should praise his daughter, I have to admit my Natasha is a good-looking girl. She has just returned after spending a month with her group, acting in East Germany and Czechoslovakia. They also spent some time in Berlin and Dresden. She is now acting here in the town and in the outskirts. Her ambition is to travel to the West but that unfortunately is not possible as yet.

Now, Jenya, I want once more to return to these distant days and the events which took place during the last few years of my sojourn in Archangel. The pattern of our life continued in the way which I have already described to you, but what was becoming more difficult to accept was the constant fear of attacks, verbal and physical, by the dreadful 'Chechenka' woman. We would have gladly moved elsewhere, but that was quite impossible as Archangel had become very overcrowded with whole families being packed into single or large rooms divided by screens, some parts with no windows and always no privacy. The adjoining corridors were packed with trunks, boxes and various belongings and in the kitchen, where there was only one tap, several housewives struggled together preparing meals for their families.

Before the start of the First World War the population was 40,000. Now it had increased five-fold. This was due not only to the influx of people from other parts of Russia, but also to the peasant population from the surrounding districts deciding to move into town after being forbidden to continue their private trading. Such was the situation. We, with our two rooms, in spite of the persecution by the 'Chechenka', had to count ourselves lucky.

I remember the winter of 1932-33 being extremely harsh, with bitter frosts and snowstorms. Dedushka continued attending the hospital, situated at the other end of the town, sometimes travelling in a crowded tramcar, or having to walk along the frozen pavements. In November of 1932 he caught a severe chill which developed into pneumonia. He became seriously ill, but our Babushka, with her usual selfless devotion nursed him day and night and by early December he recovered. Our step-grandfather, Jenya, a renowned surgeon completely devoted to his work, decided as soon as he recovered to return to the hospital. This was a tragic mistake as he again became ill and this time more seriously than before.

Undaunted, once again Babushka devoted herself completely to his recovery but this time, much weakened, Dedushka was unable to leave the house and spent his time resting.

Christmas was spent with Yura, Marga and their children. All brought presents of food. Candles were lit and we gathered round the table. A week later we were into 1933, a year that has remained vividly imprinted in my memory.

One day in late January 1933, I was sitting at Dedushka's desk engrossed in my homework. Opposite me, on my bed, Dedushka was resting and reading a book. Our peace was suddenly shattered by loud, hysterical shouting and bad language. I rushed into the corridor and met Babushka running from the kitchen with a stewpan in which was our half-cooked dinner. Behind her was the terrible 'Chechenka' waving a stick. Babushka, very upset, handed me the stewpan and asked me to put it inside the *pechka* [stove] in my room and hurried into her bedroom. The *pechka* had been heated that day and the embers were still hot. While I was placing the pot inside the pechka I heard her calling 'Put the embers . . .'

She did not finish what she was saying but I understood she meant me to place the red hot ashes round the pot. Wishing to confirm what she had said, I called to her but received no answer. I went into the bedroom. It was dark inside lit only by the lamp in front of the ikon in the corner of the room casting a soft glow.

In this half light I saw Babushka sitting on the edge of the bed in a strange position, with her right arm hanging limply by her side and her face twisted. I called to Dedushka who, after examining her, sighed heavily and quietly said, 'Babushka has had a stroke and is paralysed.' She could not speak but appeared still to have her senses about her. We put her to bed where she took Dedushka's wrist and held it in her left hand while I ran for Marga.

She died the following day. Her death shocked and saddened not only the people in the house, but all her numerous friends and even beggars whom she had helped the best way she could. Through the four years I had lived with my grandparents I never heard them exchange a single angry word. They were very special people.

On the day of the funeral Marga asked me to remain in the house with Dedushka. I led him to the window and together we watched the procession starting from the house. It was led by Anna Osipovna, better known as 'Osa'. In her hands was the large ikon of the Virgin. Behind her walked the driver leading the horse. On the ancient catafalque lay the coffin covered by the beautiful artificial flowers Babushka had at one time created and presented to her friends, who were now returning them back to her. Behind the coffin walked my father and Seryozha who had arrived from Leningrad, followed by Marga, Yura and a long train of people, many of whom, although it was snowing, walked with bared heads.

I stood with Dedushka watching this sad scene. He was constantly removing his glasses and wiping his eyes with a handkerchief in his trembling hands.

The procession on the main street gradually receded and finally turning to the right, vanished out of sight. I led Dedushka back from the window to his armchair and sat down beside him. It was Marga who took the responsibility of running the house and taking care of Dedushka. She called several times each day with food, but he never ate anything and did not touch the medicine prescribed for him. At the end of two weeks Dedushka died and was buried beside Babushka. Soon after these sad events the house was taken over by Yura and his family.

On the day after Dedushka's funeral, Marga, Seryozha and Yura arrived at the house to divide between them the articles left by my grandparents. Neither my father nor I received a single item that might have reminded us of them, but Babushka had bequeathed to me a sable-lined coat which at one time belonged to my grandfather, Aleksandr Scholts. It was a handsome coat, but not of much use to me. I toyed with the idea of passing it on to my sister Vika, as she did not have very much of anything and sable, of course, is always precious. Marga, however, took it instead, saying a sailor does not require a sable coat!

Yura who was my godfather, kindly offered to allow me to stay on in the house, but as my father, who had nowhere to go, was to continue living there, I declined Yura's offer.

Dressed in my only pair of well-worn trousers, an old jacket and cap with an anchor on it, and carrying my haversack with a change of underwear and my precious books, I left forever the house where I had spent the happiest years of my youth, and settled in the Student Hostel.

In the spring, my father having been caught in a snow storm, developed a severe chill and died. He was buried beside the other members of the family.

My young brother, Shurick, had long since left Archangel to live with Vika in Leningrad and somewhere in Ukraina was Mother and my little sister Olga from whom I never heard anything. I was the last member of the Scholts family still living in Archangel.

I have been reliving in these pages the sad events which took place during the month of my stay with our babushka and trust you will not be too upset by reading about them.

More in my next letter,

Yours as ever,

Evgenie.

Chapter 3

ARCTIC ODYSSEY

EVGENIE'S LETTERS HAD given me a deeply moving account of all that had happened after we left Russia. He was now to tell me more about his life and career.

February 1978

Dear Jenya,

We have received your welcome letter and are pleased to note all is well with your family as it is with ours. I see you have been away from home with Ronald and staying in an hotel in the country along with a group of friends whom you had known in India but who like you are now retired and living in another part of Scotland. It is a good way of keeping in touch with each other and to talk about the times you spent together in India when you were all young and life, from what you told me, was very pleasant.

I will now continue from where I left off after Babushka's death. In the spring of 1934 I received a letter from the Principal of the Sea College informing me that I had successfully passed all my final exams. I was now a fully fledged Marine Engineer. Overjoyed by my success, I imagined that my cherished hope of sailing in warm seas and visiting the lands so eloquently described by Uncle Gherman could now materialise, and that there might be a place for me on a tramp steamer. I had at times watched such ships leaving Archangel for Europe and the distant seas of the tropics.

I knew, however, that before I could travel aboard such a ship it was imperative to obtain a visa allowing me to leave Russia. Full of confidence I sent my application, but was shattered to receive a blunt refusal. I realised at once that this was due to my connections with Finland, America and Scotland. For days on end I nursed my disappointment but finally found consolation in the thought that being young another chance was bound to come along.

Meanwhile I was offered a post aboard a ship due to sail in the autumn for the Arctic regions. The name of the ship was *Gostorg*. I had already experienced such sailing aboard similar ships as during my longer summer vacations I was often given employment on ships sailing to the Arctic regions around the islands of Novaya Zemlya or Franz Josef Land. The purpose of these sailings was the killing of seals for their oil and the trapping of white bears, which were placed in special cages and taken to Murmansk from where they were sent to the various zoos in Europe.

In spite of the less pleasant tasks aboard the ships I enjoyed sailing in those regions where, during the summer months, the sun never set and where I got to know about the many rare birds and animals inhabiting the Arctic. Especially fascinating was the rare 'kasatka' – a cross between a dolphin and a whale.

On its back is a hook in the shape of a sickle with which it has been known to attack a whale and sharks are also reputed to be afraid of it. It is a vicious animal and moves at a tremendous speed. Why it is called 'kasatka' is rather strange for that is a form of endearment meaning 'darling' or 'dearie' – quite a misnomer for such a savage animal. However, I have also been told that the 'kasatka' has never been known to attack a human being.

Another species is the beluga, not to be confused with the sturgeon, the source of caviar. The beluga is a cross between a dolphin and a whale. It is enormous, white skinned, six metres long and half a ton in weight. It usually travels in shoals around the coast of Novaya Zemlya. It is reputed to have a strange, almost human cry. I have never heard it, but old sailors have assured me that they have on several occasions. It is a drawn-out, sad haunting cry which has given rise to the saying 'Crying like a beluga' often applied to someone weeping in distress.

One morning in the late autumn of 1934. I boarded the *Gostorg* where, to my joyful surprise, I met up with two of my shipmates with whom I had previously sailed in the Arctic regions. The *Gostorg* was a handsome motor-driven sailing ship, its name painted in large black letters against a white background. It was a sturdy ship built in Norway and similar in design to the one used by Nansen, the Norwegian explorer, on his Arctic expeditions.

I had imagined that there would be nothing more than the usual killing of seals and trapping of white bears, but I was mistaken. The order was to kill only the belugas as the oil of the beluga was considered to be finer than that of the seal.

The big question for us sailors was this. We knew that the belugas travelled in great shoals in the vicinity of Novaya Zemlya but when and where exactly they would appear we had no knowledge. Later, however, it transpired that information regarding this had been received from an old Samoyed [Eskimo] who lived in Novaya Zemlya. Meanwhile we talked a lot between us about this problem.

One morning when Archangel was coming back to life and the clanging of the tramcars carrying passengers on the main street to their work was heard quite clearly, *Gostorg* began slowly to move away from the pier and sail down the river. Soon we were gaining speed passing familiar places – the tree-lined boulevard, houses, the Sea College and entering the deep channel between the island of Solombala and Maimaksa . . . Goodbye Archangel!

We are accompanied by the usual 'sputniks' of all sailors – the seagulls. They circled around us, spreading their white wings, suddenly falling down and then rising again, hanging motionless in the sky.

Our crew consisted of twenty-two men and a little mongrel called 'Malchik'. We followed the usual routine with supper at 7 o'clock. Our cook, Volodya, fed us well and was in the habit of anxiously enquiring if we were satisfied with his cooking. He was not only a good cook but a talented guitarist as well and occasionally during our hours of leisure accompanied us in a sing-song. At other times some played draughts or dominoes, some read and some just sat and talked.

On the fourth day of our journey we arrived at the south point of Novaya Zemlya known as 'Karskiya Vorota' meaning 'The gateway to the Kara Sea'. The natives of this port are friendly Samoyeds to whom we were bringing a cargo of wheat, sugar grain and other products.

On hearing our siren they all rushed out of their *yurtas* [dwellings] to welcome us, their round faces expressing joy and delight for it was very rarely that ships called to their remote port. We could not loiter as it was imperative to reach Station Rusanovo, lying away to the north, before darkness fell. We lifted our anchor and the last we saw of these cheerful people was them jumping and waving their arms and we in turn were blowing our siren as a farewell gesture.

From south to north, like a long ribbon, stretches the shore of Novaya Zemlya. Nature is hard there, the summers are short with the sun never setting and over all there is the strange, haunting silence of the Arctic. In the south one can see dwarf birches, the small yellow heads of camomile, the tiny blue blossoms of some unknown species, the *moroshka* berry, the red sour *klukva* and nothing much more.

In the gathering dusk we reached Rusanovo and entered the narrow inlet to the bay where we dropped our anchor a short distance from the shore.

Rusanovo is a small station with only two single-storeyed wooden houses and a *banya* [the bath house] but further along looking like up-turned sugar basins could be seen the yurtas of some seven Samoyeds with whom we were acquainted having been there previously. From now on began the period of waiting for the arrival of the beluga.

The planned method of killing the belugas was actually quite simple. A heavy net was cast reaching from one side of the ship to the shore where it was securely fastened, thus leaving a narrow passage between the ship and the opposite shore. The beluga, chasing its prey in the shape of shoals of little fish, would enter the narrow passage only to be trapped and killed by rifle fire from the ship.

The days passed slowly with no sign of the elusive belugas. In the end the captain asked me to go ashore to consult the old samoyed who had previously assured us that this was the place the belugas came to year after year. He was an old, wise man and spoke in short clipped sentences.

'Hello Dadya,' I said to him. His flat, lined face lit up with a welcoming smile.

'Bad will be the weather,' he answered shortly, gazing into the distance and shaking his old grey head.

'Will the beluga come?' I asked him.

'When the little fish come the beluga come,' he rejoined.

'But how will the beluga know when the little fish will come?' I again asked him.

He laughed. 'Beluga knows – he wise fish – not like man. Beluga come when weather good. Weather soon no good,' he added.

I returned to the ship and reported the conversation to the captain. While we were talking, our radio operator, Vasya Trubin, knocked on the door. In his hand was a telegram from Archangel with the latest report on the weather warning us to expect a severe storm. Captain Urpin sighed deeply. 'Evgenie Aleksandrovich,' he turned to me, 'order the boys to raise the anchor and bring in the nets. We must get away from those rocks as fast as we can.'

The sailors knew that to be blown against the cliffs would be the end of the *Gostorg* and them as well. All worked with feverish speed and in a matter of two hours we were moving away from the bay in the midst of a howling gale to the safety of the open sea.

The Arctic is full of unexpected, frightening surprises. Coming towards us was a great white mass of snow almost a metre high known as a 'shuga'. It was being blown from the south and all too soon we were in the thick of it. Our speed dropped to a snail's pace. Ahead like a bright silver line the clear water of the sea, only to vanish out of sight in a blinding snowstorm and with the short day drawing to a close we were sailing in pitch darkness.

For two days and nights the struggle continued but on the third morning for a short while the blizzard abated allowing us to catch a glimpse of the shore. We discovered we were barely three miles from Station Rusanovo but again the snowstorm blotted out the view.

It was some time during that day that the mate reported to the captain that the engine had failed. Immediately we were all ordered to dress in our warmest clothing and to come on deck. This was followed by a report from our young radio operator, Vasya Trubin, always a cheerful and popular member of our crew. Now, his face white and drawn, he announced that in spite of all his efforts to transmit SOS messages to Archangel and passing ships there had been no response. Completely at the mercy of the elements we were being driven back to the shores we had left.

Straight ahead loomed a cliff as high as a three-storeyed building, coming closer with every second. Already we could see hanging from it enormous crystal icicles like threatening sentinels waiting to destroy us. We knew that if *Gostorg* struck that cliff it would be the end for the ship with all hands, but as we stood in silence awaiting our doom there occurred nothing short of a miracle – the ship cleared the rock with barely six metres to spare. We had survived, but as *Gostorg* continued racing close to the shore there came a sudden shudder, the crashing of the mast, the scattering of the crew on the frozen deck, we realised the ship had finally run aground. We were close to a small island, but with the fast-approaching darkness it was impossible to assess the situation. Through the whole of the night the ship kept shuddering, at times heeling over to the right. No one slept, wondering if *Gostorg* would eventually turn over and throw us all into the icy depths. In the pale morning light with the storm subsiding, we got our first sight of the frozen, rocky mass of the island some thirty metres high. We were barely six metres from the cliff, but with both lifeboats lost, it seemed outwith the bounds of possibility to reach the top. There was only one way and that was to shoot a line with a grapnel attached.

After several attempts we succeeded in getting the grapnel to hold on a shelf some way up the cliff. 'Who will go first?' the captain asked, and while we stood uncertainly glancing at each other, out stepped our harpoonist, Misha Plakoev. Misha, a tall man in his twenties was of a quiet disposition, always ready to listen rather than talk and was well liked and respected. Now, calmly stepping over the side and gripping the line with his hands and legs, he began to inch his way to the cliffs. Round his waist was a line the end of which was securely fixed on board.

Slowly, ignoring the icy spray from the waters below, he continued moving until he reached the shelf and from there, step by step, commenced the steep climb to the top. He moved carefully, at times halting to brush away an icicle or to test the ground for his next step. Twenty-two pairs of eyes were watching this heroic progress. We all knew that here was a man risking his life and on him depended our own salvation. When at last we saw him standing on the top and cheerfully waving his cap a great cheer went up, drowning the howling of the wind and echoing across the barren wastes of the Arctic.

The rest was simple. A strong thick rope was tied to Misha's line and hoisted to the cliff top where it was securely fixed. One by one the crew crossed over to the island and by the same means food, bundles of wood and other items worth salvaging were safely transported. Malchik, who had been pitifully whining with each departure, was placed in a bag and on reaching the top ran around joyfully barking, relieved at not being left behind. The last one to leave the ship was the captain who on arrival stood for some time looking down on the remains of his ship. The tufts of grey hair sticking below his cap, the sunken cheeks, the desolation in his eyes told their own story.

It was a small island – some thirty metres long and twenty-five across. Completely bare, with a few patches of snow and enormous boulders scattered here and there, it gave the impression of something primeval. In the summer it may have been a nesting place for birds, but now it was dead and bleak. Down below the storm had eased off but here it was blowing hard and dangerous for anyone to stand near the edge. Across the water some two kilometres from us lay Station Rusanovo. Not having any means of reaching there we hoped that someone might see us and come to our rescue.

Our captain kept scanning the shore and the sea through his binoculars but no matter how much we kept staring across, there was no sign of life. Soon daylight vanished and we were into a long dark night. A small bonfire was lit, some tins were opened and we celebrated our safe arrival. The hours that followed brought terrible hardship. With the wind dying down the frost increased, our damp clothing froze, we ran around clapping our hands and taking turns to sit beside the bonfire – it was too small for the twenty-two of us to gather round. All suffered from thirst and desperately longed to sleep but to sleep was dangerous and the captain's order was to keep moving.

At last came daybreak. Down below the storm was over; the sea was calm with the waves lazily caressing the shore. We only had three hours of daylight and already one precious hour had passed with the captain never ceasing his watch. We realised the next two hours would seal our fate. Our usually cheerful cook was sitting forlornly holding his head. His feet were frozen and he refused to move and our young sailor Egorov was showing signs of becoming very ill. We ourselves were losing our voices and talking in whispers. The thought of another night was too terrible to contemplate. The wood we brought was finished and we were already thinking of going down to bring some more from the ship when we heard the captain call out, 'I see a man with a team of dogs.' What looked at first like a dark spot, grew bigger until we also saw the man with his team of dogs. We immediately began to fire our guns, jump around, wave our hands and throw up our caps. The man halted and waved across to us. He then pointed in the direction of the Station and vanished out of sight. We realised he was away to fetch help.

Overcome by the joy of leaving this terrible island we danced around like little children with Malchik joining in our capers. Soon we made out two teams of dogs coming towards us. On each sledge was a small boat which was rowed up to the island. In one sat a Russian and on the other a Samoyed. Using a rope we descended in turn and as each boat could only carry three at a time it was a lengthy procedure. By the time we were all safely across darkness had fallen. The cook with his frozen feet was placed on one sledge and Egorov on the other. The rest of us walked. The Station lay some six kilometres from the shore. We moved slowly, at times sinking up to our knees in the snow. Weighed down by our stiff frozen clothing and with our arms stretched out we presented a picture of penguins out for a stroll. After an hour's struggling we reached the Station where we were greeted with warm hospitality. Our sick mates received medical treatment and we all sat down to a table laden with food accompanied by hot tea. Having been fed and comforted we were led to an adjoining room, heated by a *pechka*, with reindeer skins covering the floor. Thankfully we lay down and slept solidly for sixteen hours. So began our stay in Rusanovo.

Our hosts, in the house where we lived, were hunters engaged in trapping the white Polar fox as well as some other small animals. It was their custom to set off each morning with their team of dogs to a place ten kilometres from the station, where they laid the traps. The fox is an extremely cunning and sensitive animal. The traps were laid in the snow and lightly covered by the trappers wearing special gloves to prevent the fox scenting the presence of humans. Meanwhile we made ourselves useful by repairing the roof of the house which had been badly damaged by the storm. Close to the house stood an ancient deserted *izba* [cottage] built by Russians who had arrived there in distant times. There we repaired the broken *pechka* [stove], built a table and benches and used the place as a kitchen and dining-room. Below the great depth of snow lay plenty of timber. This was dug out for use in the *pechka* and the snow melted down to supply us with water.

Our main concern was the lack of provisions. It worried our cook whose problem was to provide daily meals for twenty-two men. He had limited stocks of salted beef, buckwheat, a little dried fruit, some butter, tea and dried potatoes and strict rationing had to be enforced. Each day our captain scanned the horizon in the hope of seeing a ship that might pick us up, but there was nothing to be seen. The days were passing. We formed a routine of working through the day on a variety of tasks, such as helping the trappers to skin the animals or digging in the deep snow for timber to keep our *pechka* going. In the evenings we gathered round the table. Some played cards, or homemade dominoes and some just talked. We were lucky in having saved a guitar and enjoyed musical evenings which helped to break the monotony of our existence. What worried the members of the crew was the thought that their wives, mothers and relatives would by now have come to the conclusion that the ship had perished with all hands, as there was no radio station nearby through which we might have got in touch with Archangel. We knew that scattered along the western shore up to the important station known as 'Belushiye' were huts used by Samoyed trappers. Our captain decided to try to send a letter through this chain of huts to Ilya Konstantinovich Tiko-Vilki, the Secretary of the Island Soviet who was half Samoyed and half Russian and known to be a man of great integrity. In the letter he explained our critical position and asked for a telegram to be sent to Archangel.

After three weeks of anxious waiting a letter was delivered by a trapper from Ilya Konstantinovich in Belushiye who wrote saying that he had received our letter and had sent a message to Archangel with the information that, although the ship was wrecked, all the members of the crew and their captain survived. He also strongly advised us to leave Rusanovo, where there was little chance of being picked up, and to try to reach Belushiye where ships were in the habit of calling. Incidentally, Rusanovo was the place to which I had previously been sent to ask advice from the old Samoyed, who had assured me that the 'little fish would come and the beluga would follow'. His prophecy did materialise, but we were not in a position to do any killing and even as I am writing these lines the killing of seals and whales is no longer permitted.

Between Rusanovo and Belushiye to the north lay a trek of some two hundred kilometres on the western shore of Novaya Zemlya. It was a hard, rough road exposed to all the elements of the Arctic, biting frosts, frightening storms. We had no other option but to try to reach Belushiye. There was very little food left and if it had not been for the good-natured Samoyeds who kept supplying us with fish we would have gone hungry most of the time. One evening Captain Urpin, when joining us in the dining-room, announced that he had decided to send ahead to Belushiye twelve members of the crew including myself, to be followed later by the remaining ten. We were given a fortnight to prepare during which time we had to make skis as the trappers warned us that the snowdrifts in parts were two metres in depth. We laboured hard over those skis trying to turn up the fronts by dipping the ends in boiling water and steaming them, but the wood cracked when dried. In the end there was nothing else for it but to fix strong leather straps and use the skis as they were. By the fourth of January (now 1935) the weather cleared and we were ready to start the long trek to Belushiye.

The person in charge was our boatswain, Oleg Aleksandrovich Sorokin, a tall, strong man with a personality inspiring respect. Outside the five dogs harnessed to the sleigh were waiting. The leading dog named 'Taimohr' – a highly intelligent animal – kept glancing uncertainly at her new master. All these dogs were of a mongrel breed, descendants of those originally brought from Archangel in days gone by and who throughout the years had developed thick coats enabling them to stand up to the Arctic frosts. Our Malchik, who had been in the habit of lying close to the warm *pechka*, was now unceremoniously dragged out and tethered to the team. Unaccustomed to such treatment Malchik bit the dog in front which in turn grabbed him by the throat, but a little taste of the chain soon restored order and for the whole of our difficult journey Malchik followed the team to the manner born.

On the sleigh were placed six frozen loaves of bread, salted meat and fish, tea, sugar and our guns. There was also seal meat for the dogs. We were now all set to leave Rusanovo. '*Poidyom!*' ['Let's go!'] called out our leader and to the jingling of bells and with the good wishes of our remaining friends we began the long and difficult trek to Belushiye. We followed in the footsteps of the dogs, circling round mounds and hills which added to the road but made the going easier. We travelled night and day skimming over the high snowdrifts on our home-made skis and carrying them over frozen stretches. The cold was intense but as long as we kept moving our bodies remained warm.

There were only three stations throughout the whole of our trek when we boiled snow, made tea, ate our food, fed the dogs, slept for a few hours and then once more took to the road. The further we plodded to the north the more bitter grew the frost, the harder became the road. Daylight was short but the nights were illuminated by the splendour of the northern lights casting their dazzling beams across the sky. During the last few kilometres of the journey, tormented by thirst and lack of sleep, we were in the last stage of exhaustion.

Our dogs were likewise suffering. They had with great patience and fortitude pulled the sleigh these long kilometres over rocky paths and deep snows and now with lolling tongues and bleeding paws could barely crawl.

At this point, with the ground rising ahead, we could see no sign of Belushiye and imagined that perhaps we had lost our way, but while our leader was studying his map, there came the sound of barking and we realised to our great relief that we were actually quite close to Belushiye.

We were met by a group of trappers who escorted us to Belushiye where a warm welcome awaited us from Ilya Konstantinovich Tiko-Vilki who showed us into a large room with rows of bunks and warm covers. In the adjoining room was a table laden with food, freshly baked bread, butter and milk and in the centre the purring copper samovar with the teapot sitting on top. A homely sight not seen since leaving home. Having rested and fed we were directed to the adjoining *banya* [bath house] furnished with forms, tubs, soap and an abundance of hot water. Later, after wallowing in such luxury, we retired to our bunks with the happy thought that there would be no trekking tomorrow. There was a certain satisfaction in realising that badly clad, poorly shod and tormented by thirst and hunger, we had traversed those one hundred and forty kilometres, through storms and bitter frosts, on our home-made skis and in the end defeated the Arctic.

Belushiye, although an important centre, was not unlike Rusanovo. There were two large houses occupied by the locals and us, a bath house, a large shed for dogs, a few outhouses and some distance away the round *yurtas* [tents covered in deerskin] where lived the Samoyeds.

As in Rusanovo, we made ourselves useful by repairing roofs, overhauling engines, and building two small rowing boats required by the inhabitants. Time was passing, the days grew longer and in March Captain Urpin arrived with the remainder of our crew. Their trek had been hard, all were exhausted, but with the warmer weather they had escaped the biting frosts and snowstorms.

The old routine was once again established. Each one in turn prepared breakfast, set the table, cut the bread, heated the samovar and at night gathered to play cards, dominoes, have long discussions or sing songs to the accompaniment of the old guitar. Each day we scanned the sea in the hope of spotting the promised ship but so far there was no sign of it.

One morning we were awakened by the joyful chirping of a large flock of *punochkis* [the tiny Arctic sparrows] who had landed on our window sills. With grains and bread crumbs we went out to welcome these little messengers of spring, but could not make them stay and after a day of rest they continued their flight to the north. Other feathered guests followed. Great flocks of geese accompanied by their shrill cackling flew overhead also hurrying north. 'A couple of roasted geese would be a fine change from the salted beef,' remarked our cook watching their flight – 'but who would want to kill them after their long journey home?' he added somewhat wistfully.

Spring in the Arctic is somewhat rather special. Gone is all darkness and the emerald waves serenely lap the rocky shores. The earth, no longer fettered by frosts and snow, comes to life again and is soon carpeted by masses of tiny flowers in all the hues of the rainbow. Over all lies a deep enchanting silence undisturbed by any harsh sounds such as on the mainland.

One morning in June it was my turn to set the breakfast table, cut the bread and heat the samovar. Having finished my chores I was sitting outside on an upturned bucket with Malchik at my feet enjoying the lovely morning and being at peace with the world when suddenly I heard the familiar steady beat of a ship's engine and realised the long-awaited rescue was at hand. I immediately ran to awaken my sleeping mates with the good news, but they, thinking at first it was a joke on my part, pelted me with their pillows and shoes. Soon, however, we were all on the pier, welcoming the arrival of the ship. It turned out to be the sister ship of our ill-fated *Gostorg*, named *Murmanets* and had arrived from Murmansk. We were acquainted with several members of the crew, some of whom at one time had sailed aboard the *Gostorg* and were anxious to hear the tragic details of the disastrous end of our ship and our amazing survival.

Not much time was wasted on gathering our few belongings and soon we were aboard the *Murmanets* waving our goodbyes to all our friends who had come to see us off. They were all there – the trappers, the locals, the Samoyeds and Ilya Konstantinovich Tiko-Vilko who had made our journey possible.

The last sight I remember of Belushiye was that of our poor Malchik running up and down the dock and pitifully howling his head off. We had all gone in a body to beg the captain to allow our faithful Malchik to be brought aboard, but the captain, who did not approve of dogs travelling on ships, rejected our plea.

'Malchik,' he said, 'will settle down with the other dogs and will make a good member of the team' – and so on this sad note we left Belushiye. Three days later we were in Murmansk.

Most of the crew went on to Archangel but I, not certain as to where I would be staying, decided to remain with the others in Murmansk. From there, for the next two years I continued sailing on various ships, at times on trawlers fishing around the White Sea and the coast of Murmansk or on ships carrying passengers to the islands and occasionally to Leningrad where I was always welcomed by Victoria.

Later, in the years to come after my marriage, Leningrad became my second home. I trust, dear Jenya, you have found this lengthy account of our disaster in Novaya Zemlya of some interest.

It is some time since I have heard from you but I am hoping that in the near future I shall see the familiar envelope.

With love to you all

Evgenie

August 1978

Dear Jenya,

At last your long awaited letter has arrived. Judging by the postmark it has been on the road for four weeks. The envelope, badly torn, was stuck together yet inside everything appeared to be in order. We are all very interested in the copies of the old photographs of the family in the garden. Thank you also for all the information regarding our distant ancestors and the interesting accounts of events connected with them.

Being very young I have no recollection of anyone referring to the past. I remember, however, Babushka describing an interesting journey with her mother to St Petersburg on a troika in the dead of winter, but she never explained the purpose of that journey and now you tell me it was to beg the Tsar Alexsandr II to free our grandfather from Siberia where he was serving a term for accidentally killing a soldier. I can understand the reason for her reticence.

Regarding your query about Marga – I have to explain that during my sailing trips in the Arctic regions and staying first in Murmansk, then in Leningrad, I lost touch with my relatives and friends in Archangel, but later in 1937 decided to visit my home town. Shortly before my departure, Uncle Seroyzha told me that he had received a letter from Archangel containing the tragic news of the arrest and execution of Marga's husband, Dmitry Danilov. Dmitry, who worked in the office which issued ration cards, was accused of stealing those cards and at that time anyone found guilty of such a crime was sentenced to be shot.

Dmitry Danilov and Aunt Marga with their three children lived on the top floor of a spacious house situated not far from our own in Uspenskaya Street. I often visited them and always received a warm welcome. Aunt Marga in turn with her children used to call on us. She was very kind to Uncle Gherman and liked to have long discussions with him. Dmitry was a tall, handsome giant, flaxen haired with blue eyes and fine features. He reminded one of a Russian *'bogatir'* [knight] straight out of an old Russian fairy tale. His strength was prodigious which at times he displayed by grasping with one hand the leg of a heavy armchair and raising it high above his head, a sight which never failed to delight us children.

The Danilov family stemmed from a hard-working peasant ancestry. Dmitry owned the house where he and Marga lived with their family. After it was confiscated, as were all privately owned houses, they were still allowed to live on the top floor, for which they considered themselves very lucky as so many other families were just thrown out on to the street.

And so one morning in the autumn of 1937, after an absence of three years, I arrived by ship in my home town and set off for Kuznichiha which, as you know, is the district in the north of the city where my mother's brother, Uncle Andrei, lived with his wife Nastya. Both welcomed me with open arms.

Aunt Nastya had prepared a lovely *pirog* with salmon [a fish pasty] and many other Archangel specialities which I had not seen for many years. I spent a week with my uncle and aunt, during which I set off one morning to call on Uncle Yura and, if possible, find Aunt Marga.

Although the names of the streets were changed, everything seemed to be much the same – if anything more shabby and somehow sad. While passing our own familiar street, I halted beside the house where I was born and spent my childhood. I stood there staring up at the window of the room I shared at one time with Uncle Gherman. The glass was broken; the house appeared to be empty with the gate hanging askew.

At the other end of the town was the Pomorskaya Street, still bearing its old name on the corner of which stood the house where I spent my happiest years when living with my grandparents. It had remained unchanged. Uncle Yura, who took the house over after their death, was still living there with his wife Manya and young son Alexei. Uncle Yura, as you will remember, was my godfather and some of my brightest memories are of those distant days when I used to accompany him and his dog on his hunting expeditions, during which we spent long happy hours wandering in the woods and, at the end of the day, arrived back with the bounty of a few partridges and an occasional capercaillie, a most welcome addition to our meagre diet.

I looked forward to meeting him again, but after climbing the old familiar stairs and ringing the bell, a pleasant-faced woman who shared the flat informed me that Yura was at present in Siberia and his wife, with young Alexei, was visiting her mother. Uncle Yura worked for the government department engaged in fur trading with the West. His work took him to many parts in the extreme north and Siberia, involving days of endless travelling on rough roads by horse and sledge in the dead of winter or on a peasant's cart in summer. He had to deal with trappers and breeders of valuable animals such as sable, mink and silver fox, the skins of which brought a rich reward to the government.

Although disappointed at not seeing Yura, I consoled myself with the thought that I was bound to revisit Archangel and would meet with him again.

There was still Aunt Marga. I was determined to find her, but in spite of all my enquiries no one appeared to know where she had gone. In the end I called on the people who were at one time her neighbours and they were able to tell me that they had heard she was now living on the outskirts of the city in one of the cottages situated beside the ancient monastery of St Michael. I went to this place and found the cottages standing a short distance from the shore of the river. Most of those wooden cottages were derelict, with blank spaces for windows and surrounded by broken fencing. There was no sign of life and over all lay the silence of the grave. I wandered around for some time in growing darkness with the cold autumn rain beating on my face, and at long last found three cottages in a row which appeared to be occupied.

Not knowing which might be Marga's, I knocked hopefully at the door of the cottage in the middle. 'Who is there?' I heard a nervous voice, and, immediately recognising it as Marga's, answered, 'It's me – Evgenie'. The door opened, and standing on the threshold was my aunt. For a few seconds I was taken aback. A mere three years ago I remembered seeing a tall, handsome woman, still in her thirties, with dark, curly hair, rosy-cheeked, bright-eyed, and now standing before me was the shrunken figure of an old woman, her face wrinkled, hollow-eyed, and the loosely hanging hair completely white. 'Evgenie – dear Jenchick,' Marga cried, bursting into tears and throwing her arms around me. She led me through a narrow passage into a small kitchen, with the usual Russian *pechka* [stove] reaching almost to the ceiling. Sitting on top was a good-looking, red-headed little boy who made a funny face at me and promptly ducked down out of sight! He was Marga's youngest child, Nikolai, or Kolya, aged five.

The kitchen was sparsely furnished with a table and three chairs. In a small adjoining room was a bed, a chest of drawers with a mirror on top, a trunk, and a few cardboard boxes. On the window-sill stood a tumbler with faded flowers. Everything spoke of great want and poverty. I sat down at the table. Marga, after preparing the samovar, removed from her trunk the last letter written by her husband and, sitting beside me, asked me to read it to her. In this short letter smuggled from the prison on the eve of his execution, Dmitry wrote the following words which are still engraved in my memory: 'My dearest Margochka, I am on the threshold of my death and I know you will believe me when I tell you – I am quite innocent. Take care of our children – pray for me. God bless you. Your loving husband, Dmitry.'

'Yes, he was innocent, completely innocent,' Marga confirmed, weeping bitterly. 'Dmitry would never have stolen anything. He was not a thief. They took him away, I never saw him again and, as if that was not enough, they came back the next day and threw me and my children out of the house just as we were. They confiscated everything, all our belongings and even Kolya's toys,' she added sadly.

'No one helped us. People were afraid to help. We ran to Sashenka – you remember her – she was a teacher who used to come every day to your babushka's house. She took us in and we stayed there for a short time, but then she was also in trouble and again we had nowhere to go; but not everyone was afraid. I still had friends who helped me to find this cottage and gathered some furniture such as this table and chairs and the samovar. We have a roof over our heads but only God knows for how long,' she concluded.

By now the samovar was singing a welcoming song. Marga placed it on the table and cut some bread. I had brought a packet of tea and a jar of honey. Little Kolya came down from his warm nest on the pechka and shyly joined us at the table. Soon Liza arrived from school. She was Marga's oldest child and was now fifteen years of age – a good-looking girl, fair-haired, blue-eyed like her father. She was also very cheerful and brightened us up with her lively chatter. I never met Marga's son Volodya, who was then thirteen years old, but heard Liza tell her mother that 'Volodya was off with the boys'.

We spent a long time at the table reminiscing with Liza listening to the stories of happier days. It was late when I kissed them goodbye and set off on the long road back. I left with a heavy heart, tormented by my helplessness and the fear that the whole situation was uncertain, and that perhaps more trouble was still in store for Marga.

The moon was high, lighting up the dreary expanse with the derelict huts and the ancient monastery of St Michael in the background. Down below, the Dvina, bright as silver, indifferent to the joys and sorrows of the people on her shores, still flowed serenely on her way to the sea.

I was fortunate to reach the terminal in time to catch the last tramcar, which took me back to Kuznechiha at the other end of the town.

The following day, I set off for the cemetery to pay my respects to the graves of my relatives. Suspecting that they might require attention, I took some tools with me. The cemetery was indeed badly neglected, all the paths being overgrown by tall, dry grass, thistles and nettles. Our own piece of ground, surrounded by broken railings, was in the same sad state of neglect. In the foreground were the two graves, close together, of our babushka and step-grandfather, and beyond could be seen those of my father and Uncle Gherman. A young rowan tree had sprung up over the years behind my uncle's grave, with a few clusters of scarlet berries still clinging to the branches. Away to the left were the two imposing gravestones in red granite, looking a little incongruous behind the plain wooden crosses. On the first could be read the names of our Scholts ancestors dating back to the end of the eighteenth century, and on the second the name of our grandfather, first husband of Babushka – Aleksandr Robert Scholts – 1848 to 1890. Sad to say, this monument had been vandalised with the top broken off and lying on the ground.

I laboured hard all day, clearing the paths and tending the graves, accompanied by the cheerful chirping of a little bird in the rowan tree. The short autumn day was drawing to a close as I was clearing up the last of the graves. It was time to call it a day. For a few moments I stood surveying the scene, remembering all those who at one time were a part of my life but were now at peace, untouched by the present fears and anxieties.

Content with my day's work, I made my way back to the warmth of my aunt's house. My short holiday was now drawing to a close, but prior to leaving Archangel, I was anxious to pay a visit to Babushka's old garden where I had spent so many happy hours in my childhood.

The house still stood on the corner of the river front and Olonetskaya Ulitza, now renamed Ulitza Gaidara, but was barely recognisable – grey, dingy coloured, in poor condition, it was now used as a children's hospital. The adjoining double gates were securely locked, not a soul was to be seen to open it and let me in.

Through the bars of the gate I could see that the hedge separating the courtyard from the garden was removed with the few trees still standing obscuring the view beyond. Disappointed, I turned away. The steps beside the house took me on to the river front. The Dvina, beautiful as ever, was very still with not a ripple to be seen. The first touch of frost was in the air and perhaps she was already preparing herself for the approaching long winter sleep. The tall birches lining the avenue were discarding their summer garb. The dried, reddish leaves rustled underfoot. Nearby, across from the avenue, was the fine old building of the Sea School. I crossed over and stood watching the noisy throng of future sailors hurrying out of the gates, reminding me of my happy days spent there. I was happy to note that the school was the same as on the day when I left it, but further along, changes had taken place, with many privately owned, handsome houses removed and replaced by mediocre buildings. I should like to have seen some more of the river front and the town itself, but my time was running out. The following day I said 'goodbye' to my hospitable aunt and uncle and boarded the ship for Leningrad.

Soon after my arrival in Leningrad my fears about Marga were confirmed when we received a letter from Archangel with the distressing news that she had been sent to a district known as Kami situated to the south-east from Archangel. Her young daughter Liza voluntarily followed so as to be near her mother. For a few years Marga survived, but in the end lost her reason and died there. For a long time we never knew what had happened to the two boys but after the war received the scanty information that Vladimir had committed suicide and his young brother, the red-headed Kolya, was killed in an accident. Such was the tragic end of the family with only Liza being spared. After her mother's death she still continued living in the same district where she eventually married and settled down. From all accounts she corresponds with her cousin Nina who, like herself, is the sole survivor of Uncle Seryozha's family.

Soon after receiving the sad news about Marga, I was back at sea, sailing on a fishing trawler for a year and more in the stormy Arctic waters with my base in Murmansk and it was there I found a letter awaiting me from Victoria in which she informed me that Yura, our step-uncle who was also my godfather, had committed suicide by shooting himself. I found it difficult to accept such terrible news. Uncle Yura, still in his thirties, happily married, life-loving and enjoying his work, was the last man to contemplate suicide.

It so happened that shortly after receiving this devastating news, my ship called at Archangel. I took this opportunity to call on Manya, his widow, who was still living in the house with her young son Alesha. Manya happened to be out but the neighbours told me how, on that tragic day, they suddenly heard the sound of a shot which appeared to come from Yura's room. They found him sitting in his armchair, slumped forward, his head on the desk and lying beside him was his shotgun. When I met Manya later, she told me she believed there was some trouble in connection with Yura's work and that someone was trying to squeeze him out. He was worried by the thought that perhaps he would lose his job.

Somehow this explanation did not sound true to me. I had the horrible suspicion that the trouble with his work was a prelude to something far worse than the loss of his job. There was a reason but what it was I could not fathom. I have to add that the thirties were the most frightening and difficult years of our time. I was glad to be at sea, away from all the intrigues and reprisals that went on.

I feel this has been a very long letter with too many accounts of unhappy events. I shall try to write in a more cheerful vein in my

future letters. I am looking forward to your reply.
With love and best wishes to you and your family
Evgenie

Author's Note

At this point I should like to add that I believe I know the reason why our Uncle Yura took his own life. I have to go back to the year of 1918 – the time when the great Allied Intervention took place, an intervention I consider to be the greatest blunder of the whole of the First World War, paid for by a great loss of life, not only Russian, but of the Allies as well, especially the British, and in the end a complete failure resulting in a shameful departure leaving the Russian Democratic forces diminished in numbers, short of ammunition, to fight on alone. Defeat was inevitable and brought, under Communist rule, unspeakable suffering lasting more than seventy long years.

My cousin Evgenie, or Jenchik, as he was known in his early years, was born in 1914 and therefore too young to remember the stirring events which took place during his early childhood. I, being eight years older, had the advantage of remembering the advent of the Democratic Revolution in March 1917, followed by the illegal usurping of power by Lenin and the establishing of the Bolsheviks in numerous cities, including Archangel, lasting until that glorious day, when strong underground forces chased them out of the town and up the river. They fled in every type of boat on which they could lay their hands. The red rag was torn down and the old national flag was once again fluttering over the town hall, all set to welcome the great armada.

How wonderful was the sight of those beautiful ships, sailing proudly, silhouetted against the golden light of the setting sun. How joyful was the welcome and how sad it was a mere year later to see them in the early morning, slinking quietly away, never to return, and hearing Uncle Seryozha say, 'Why did they come? We shall pay dearly for this!'

Meanwhile, during the start of the Intervention, in early August of 1918, Uncle Yura and his friend Dmitry Danilov were schoolboys attending the Lomonosov Gymnasium but in early 1919, after completing their education and abandoning all hopes of joining the University of St Petersburg, they, and many other young men, joined what was known as the Russo-British Legion. I remember how handsome they looked in their British officers' uniforms, complete with the Sam Browne belt with shoulder strap! The Legion took part in many bitter battles against the Bolshevik forces. The final and desperate battle took place in February 1920, outside Archangel. The Russians, now on their own and with hardly any ammunition, fought bravely until the inevitable defeat, which was followed by executions and imprisonment. Dmitry Danilov succeeded in escaping and hiding in the woods. Yura was arrested and imprisoned in the local prison but eventually spared by the entreaties of his soldiers on his behalf.

There is no doubt that in the secret files of the K.G.B. were the names of all the officers who fought against communism and especially that of Yura, who had been decorated for an act of bravery when at the risk of his life he had extinguished the fuse of a bomb set to blow up an important bridge on the railway. Throughout the monstrous reign of Stalin, and especially during the thirties, some twenty million people were executed including many former officers of the White Army who had led blameless lives since the end of the Civil War. The fact that both Dmitry and Yura were members of the Slavo-British Legion must have aroused some attention. The usual procedure was to lodge a false charge followed by interrogation and execution. After Dmitry's death, Yura, realising what was in store for him, forestalled them!

June 1979

Dear Jenya,

This morning I received a joyful surprise in the shape of an unexpected letter from you. I was sitting at my desk working on a model of an ancient sailing ship that used to be displayed in Archangel. This is my favourite hobby and helps to pass away the time. Close beside me was our cat Yashka, watching intently all my movements in the hope that I might decide to take him for a walk. He is a funny cat, our Yashka, and likes nothing better than to accompany Elena and me when we go for a stroll. Unlike a dog he does not run close beside us but keeps vanishing and reappearing and in the end is usually found sitting waiting for us on our doorstep. He always knows when there is someone at the door and this time, suddenly jumping down and hurrying to it, whom did he find but our little elderly postwoman, standing smiling, with a bulky letter in her hand! She is a little bit short-sighted and at times places the letter in the wrong postbox, but today had decided to deliver it in person.

Inside your letter were many interesting pictures, old and new and taken at various times and different places. We particularly liked the one of you standing beside the portrait of yourself taken when you were only eleven. I shall arrange them all in my special album in which I began to place all the pictures you have sent me from that day in 1972 when we began our correspondence. At times, when writing to you, I open the album and read your letters over again and in those moments I feel as if we are sitting together and you are describing all these amazing events which took place in the distant past, about which, being so young, I knew nothing at all. I am reminded how, on one occasion, our babushka described to me her amazing journey in the dead of winter from Archangel to St Petersburg in the year 1880, but when I asked her what was the reason for such a difficult journey, she merely replied 'business on behalf of your grandfather'. Now I know the reason was to beg Alexsandr II to pardon our grandfather who had been involved in the death of a soldier.

We are now into late June. It has been so far a pleasant summer with the long daylight, well into the night, which appeals to me as it reminds me of the 'White Nights' of Archangel. Yesterday – the 20th of June – was Trinity Sunday. It is a day when some of our citizens make a point of visiting the cemeteries where their loved ones are buried.

In the morning Elena and I, together with Natasha and Seryozha, boarded a tramcar and after some twenty-five minutes arrived at Ohtinskoye cemetery where are buried Elena's relatives, including her mother who had died from starvation during the siege of Leningrad. After paying our respects we left and, travelling once more by tramcar, duly arrived at the Finnish Station from where the electric train took us to the Pargolovo cemetery to pay homage at my mother's grave.

This is a spacious, well-laid-out cemetery with plenty of greenery and flowers against the background of tall young birches. There are tidy paths and wooden forms for those who may wish to rest their weary feet and each grave is kept in perfect order. There are no churches. At the entrance we are met by a long row of sellers offering a great variety of flowers and bouquets of all sizes. Inside we find a great mass of people. They have arrived with bags of provisions, some carrying folding chairs and little tables. On arriving at the grave of their loved ones, they settle down and proceed to lay out all the delectable eats along with a bottle of wine or vodka. They will drink to the memory of the dear departed and if by chance he or she likewise enjoyed a drink during their lifetime, a small glass of vodka and a little *zakuska* is placed on the grave. Later we all stroll around meeting old friends, exchanging news, holding long conversations and, in the end, leave for home, having spent a pleasant day. This kind of homage occurs every year. Having spent my youth in Archangel, I had never seen anything like those yearly gatherings. In Archangel, we arrive at the cemetery, tidy the grave, place some flowers, pay our silent respects and depart. Neither do we ever have photographs of the deceased, placed in glass frames above the grave such as is often seen here. To me this is rather strange and in any event would not survive our Arctic conditions. I am expecting my brother Shurick to arrive from

Moscow, where he lives with his wife, son and daughter. We are planning to spend a week with Vika in the country, where she has bought a cottage and loves to potter about in her garden. She has asked me to thank you for the seeds you sent her. They have all taken and she is expecting a fine crop of vegetables.

I will close meantime. Elena sends her love. Write! Please write!

Evgenie

August, 1980

Dear Jenya,

Here I am once again! I was hoping on my return from the country to find the familiar envelope, but had no such luck! I live in hope!

Meanwhile I shall describe our visit to Vika's cottage. Many people in Leningrad own such cottages in the country and go there for their holidays to get away from what they believe is the unhealthy atmosphere and heat of the summer in Leningrad which they maintain is especially bad for children. Our Seryozha has received permission to build one for himself but progress is slow due to scarcity of materials and lack of transport. These cottages are only occupied during the summer months as in winter the wells are frozen, fuel is not always available and therefore they are not habitable. The main purpose of our visit was to help Vika with the repairs to the roof of her cottage. Shurick duly arrived from Moscow and the two of us set off for the country. First there was the journey by the Metro, followed by a bus which took us to the point from where we had to walk over several fields until we reached Vika's cottage. She and her husband own a large piece of ground, where they grow a great variety of vegetables and berries and also have a few apple trees. The cottage contains a spacious living-room, two bedrooms and a kitchen. Beside the cottage is a *banya* [bath house] complete with *pechka* [stove] and wooden benches. We spent a busy time helping Vika's husband, Kyrill, to repair the roof. Vika and her husband are not in the best of health these days and were duly grateful for our assistance. Later Shurick and I enjoyed a session in the *banya*, where Vika had heated the *pechka* and had filled two barrels, one with hot water and the other with ice-cold water from the well. There was also laid out a bunch of birch twigs with which to beat ourselves, a health-giving exercise! After the *banya* we joined Vika and Kyrill round the samovar and there was this wonderful feeling of well-being which I had to admit can never be experienced after a normal bath or shower. We drank endless glasses of tea, accompanied by home-made raspberry jam and talked well into the night, recalling our sad childhood when we were scattered between relatives and friends but somehow always kept in touch with each other and were now, in our old age, sitting together. Only Olga, our little sister, now living in far-off America, was absent. Although I correspond with her, I know I shall never see her again.

I was happy to note that you both continue to exchange letters, as I suspect that at times she must feel lonely and perhaps regrets that she is not back in Russia, close to her own family.

I will close on this sad note. Elena joins with me in sending our best wishes to you and Ron and all the family.

With love,
Evgenie

September, 1980

Dear Jenya,

There has been no sign as yet of the familiar envelope but last week we received your postcard from England where you were spending a few days with Michael and his family and yesterday our postwoman delivered a large parcel addressed to Natasha. We got in touch with her and she arrived in the evening. Inside was the beautiful flame-coloured evening dress. She is delighted and very grateful. A dress such as this one would be quite impossible to find here.

The measurements you sent for turned out to be a perfect fit and Natasha will be writing to you. She is especially glad to receive this dress as she is acting in a revue due to take place in Leningrad at the start of the New Year which Elena and I hope to attend. It is very rare that we have the chance to see our daughter on the stage, for as I have mentioned before most of the time her group performs all over Russia and in countries within our political group such as East Germany, Rumania, Bulgaria and so on.

Elena and I have decided to visit some places of interest such as Peterhof, Pushkino and others in the outskirts of Leningrad. We hope to do this before the real autumn takes over. At present it is still warm and sunny and quite pleasant for a stroll in our parks – we hope it will continue although already there is the smell of autumn in the air.

I will close meanwhile. We send our best regards to Ronald and to all the children and grandchildren. I kiss and embrace you. Please write!

Evgenie

A memorable picnic on the Dvina. Our hostess, Mrs Sevestianov, made a hat out of paper napkins to keep the sun off my head!

Tea with Mrs Gemp – a remarkable lady who has led thirty expeditions around the White, Baltic and Kara Seas.

Family gathering in St Petersburg, 1990. *(Above, left to right)* Elena, the author, Shurick, Michael, Seryozha, Elena, Aleksandr, Rodion. *(Below)* The same group with my cousin's daughter Natasha shown on the right between her husband Jenya and son Aleksandr.

Farewell party in Archangel, 1990 with all our friends.

With Tanya in the mayor's office, Archangel, 1992.

'Only the Dvina remains . . . .'

January, 1981

Dear Jenya,

At last your long-awaited letter has arrived. I have to admit I was rather anxious and wondered if all was well, but fully understand that moving to another house and having to create some order absorbs a lot of time. I note it is a smaller house, but in a very pleasant part of the city with easy access to shopping. You say you are missing your lovely garden and the one in front of the house is very small, but that perhaps is not such a drawback for although I believe you are a very energetic woman, you will not always be so, and a large garden could turn out to be a heavy burden.

We are a bit younger, but I can tell you that our little lemon tree and the flowers in the balcony are more than enough for us to cope with. I was pleased and interested to know that George helped with the decorations and tiled the kitchen. That requires a pair of clever hands which he must have. As you know he is the one in your family whom I met away back in 1962 when he was with a group of students on a cultural mission to Russia. How well I remember that happy evening when we all gathered in Vika's house. Our neighbour, who spoke English, acted as an interpreter. Later I accompanied George to his hotel and although there was the problem with the language, we somehow understood each other. I remember recognising you in his features and wishing I could have seen him again but he was leaving for Kiev the following day. That was the only time I met your son. 'Strange are the ways of our Lord' goes the Russian saying. Jenya, who could have ever imagined that one day I and my Uncle Gherman's grandson would be walking together along the streets of Leningrad? Please give George my regards and tell him that I still remember our happy meeting. I know that the house will keep you busy for some time, but please write when you have a moment to spare.

Elena and I wish you all the best in your new surroundings.

Evgenie

97

Chapter 4

THE FINAL LETTERS

WE HAD NOW been corresponding for nine years and in these final letters Evgenie brought me up to date with the present generation of the family.

March 1981

Dear Jenya,

Thank you for your ever welcome letter. I am pleased to know that all the various alterations in the kitchen have been completed and that you now have more time to yourself. I was interested to read that for some years you have been writing your memoirs and had attended evening lectures on literature in Edinburgh University where one of the professors, after reading an extract you had submitted to him, advised you to continue writing. You have never mentioned this to me before. I am astonished and delighted; you certainly must continue, as apart from having a remarkable memory, your descriptions of all the distant events of which I knew nothing at all, have a vivid style – just as if it all happened yesterday! You write of course in English and how sorry I am that I do not know that language. I think I know from whom you inherit this gift for I remember my father telling me that Uncle Gherman, as a young man, often submitted short stories to the *Severnoye Utro* [*Northern Morning*], a well-known newspaper in Archangel, which were always accepted. I rather think he would have continued had he not lost his eyesight. Yes, you must continue and who knows, all these reminiscences might make an interesting book.

Last week Elena and I attended the revue in which Natasha was taking part. It was held in the theatre 'Estrada', one of the oldest theatres in Leningrad, situated near the Nevsky Prospect. We were sitting in the middle of the second row and, although a bit excited, tried to appear calm and composed. I remember thinking how good it might have been if you had been sitting beside us.

First, there were separate acts, presenting singing, dancing, a short play, followed by the compère, announcing – 'And now please welcome our own lovely Nataliya Rostovskaya.' To the sound of music and loud applause our daughter took the stage. I have to admit, Jenya, she is a good-looking girl, and dressed in that lovely flame-coloured dress, golden slippers, her fair hair hanging loosely down to her shoulders, she was beautiful!

Accompanied by the orchestra she sang, danced and told stories, at times sad, at times humorous. I had never realised before how truly talented she is. She carried the audience with her and at the end received deafening applause which continued until she appeared once more and presented another short act. We were both immensely proud of our daughter and felt rewarded after all the hardship and difficulties we went through in those past years when bringing up our children.

I do not know from whom our Natasha takes this talent, but think it must run in the Scholts family. Our babushka was a talented gardener and designed her own unique garden, such as Archangel never had before and will never see again. She also created exquisite, almost life-like flowers.

Then there was Adya, our fathers' cousin. Do you remember him? After the timber mills were confiscated, he and his wife, Natasha, went on the stage. He was a very good actor as was his wife. They both performed in Leningrad and travelled with a group all over Russia but later, during the thirties, Adya was arrested and sent to Siberia where he died. His wife Natasha continued living in Leningrad until she died some years ago. They had a son called Aleksander who was also talented and acted in what was known as 'The Children's Theatre'. I once met him but have long since lost touch although I believe he must be still living somewhere in Leningrad. I must stop now. Our regards to Ron and the family.

Please write and continue your reminiscences. I kiss and embrace you.

Evgenie

May, 1981

Dear Jenya,

Thank you very much for your letter and my birthday gift which arrived this morning. I am delighted to receive this lovely scarf of such excellent quality and unusual design. You tell me the colours and pattern represent the Fraser clan. I have read about the different clans whose origins are in the hills of Scotland, but I did not know before that each clan had its own particular tartan nor did I know that the

Frasers originally came from Normandy. I am always learning and shall be proud to wear it. I note you have been away to the town of Dundee attending a wedding of the daughter of an old friend whom you knew in India. I was interested to note that it was a church wedding followed by a reception and dancing well into the night. Church weddings are very rare here and usually not much time is wasted on receptions.

When our Seryozha was married, the wedding took place in what is known as 'The Hall of Weddings'. There are a few of them scattered throughout Leningrad. I am enclosing in this letter the picture of Seryozha and his bride Elena taken on the day of their wedding in 1976. The hall we chose was quite impressive. Inside was a magnificent marble staircase, the walls lined with gilded mirrors, everything sparkling and in the background soft music: upstairs is an equally sumptuous, spacious hall with gilded chairs and crystal chandeliers. Relatives and friends sit in the background and the young couple walk up to a table where a lady is sitting. She asks a few questions, after which they sign a paper or two and are then considered to be married. After this brief ceremony you are directed to the reception room. There the table is spread with a variety of zakuskis, chocolates and fruit with wine and champagne served in crystal goblets. Everyone gathers round but no one sits down. We drink to the health of the newly-weds, give a few speeches and the whole reception is over in less than an hour.

Following the reception, the young couple, along with the bride's mother, Natasha and my Elena's sister returned to the house, where Elena had earlier prepared a cold buffet accompanied by wine and vodka. We gathered round and it was all very pleasant, but had to be cut short as Seryozha and his bride were booked on the train to the Crimea where they planned to spend their honeymoon – on the beautiful shores of the Black Sea. This wedding I may add cost me 600 roubles [£400] which included the price of the gold wedding ring and a suit.

Natasha, who was married in 1973, paid for her own wedding as she was earning far more than my pension and I was only able to give her 150 roubles [£100]. We did, however, prepare a good reception which was attended by our close relatives. On the table were flowers, a selection of cold dishes, champagne and vodka.

Our children, I may add, know nothing about religious wedding services, never having been taught religion in their schools. Elena occasionally goes to church, but I have never attended any church service since I left Archangel. I should like to talk to you a little longer and ask more questions, but I am due to go to the eye hospital to have my eyes examined. They have been bothering me lately – I think perhaps I am requiring new glasses.

I will close meantime. Our regards to Ron and the family.

I embrace and kiss you.

Evgenie

August 1981

Dear Jenya,

Thank you for your letter. It has taken only seven days to arrive which is nothing short of miraculous: I note you have been staying with Michael and his family in a village near the town of Bristol in England where he has a nice house and garden. I note he is periodically moved around, but if that means promotion, perhaps it is all for the best. I was interested to read that recently you had Leo, our late cousin Marina's son, staying with you. You know, I met him some years ago when he arrived from Finland with a group of tourists in Leningrad. Marina, sadly, was dead by that time. I found Leo a very friendly young man, but conversation was difficult, as, unlike George, he did not know a single word of Russian and I, likewise, knew not one word of Finnish, which is considered to be a very difficult language.

I recollect our babushka, who corresponded with Aunt Olga, telling me that when Leo was an infant, he soon discovered that no matter how loudly he cried his mother would not hear him and the only way to attract her attention was to crawl up to her and pull her skirt! Marina's husband was also deaf but in each case it was not hereditary, and Leo actually turned out to be very musical. You tell me he is now married and has a lovely fair-haired daughter whom he adores and keeps sending you pictures of her since her early childhood. It is sad that Marina never had the joy of seeing her granddaughter.

Here nothing unusual has been happening. Elena keeps the house – I do all the shopping. From what I can gather our prices of food overall are much the same as in Britain with the exception of bread which is six times dearer than in Russia. What is far more expensive here and nothing like the quality abroad is clothing and shoes. A suit or a coat will cost more than twice our pension! Meat, pork, chickens, ducks are usually available and I believe a little cheaper than in Europe, as is fish when available, but good fish is very rare and whenever I hear of cod or '*lintai*' – a fish resembling cod but not so good – I rush off and bring as much as I can carry. Also, when I have the chance to buy a good cut of beef, I will buy two or three kilos and carry everything back and place it in our fridge, but in the winter we also store food on our balcony.

Usually when I finish the shopping, I stop on my way home at a kiosk and drink a glass of '*kvaas*' – a very refreshing home-made brew from black bread and raisins. Neither Elena nor I drinks very much, only an occasional glass or two of vodka and that when celebrating something special or entertaining friends. I still attend the eye clinic where I receive treatment and special drops, something they say I have to continue with to avoid losing my eyesight, a prospect I certainly do not relish. Our summer is drawing to a close, but the weather is still pleasant for Elena and I do enjoy our walks in the nearby, as yet unspoiled, surroundings.

I will close now and will await your next letter. You have no idea how much pleasure I derive from them. I trust you are continuing with your reminiscences.

I kiss and embrace you. Elena sends her regards.

Evgenie

October 1981

Dear Jenya,

Many thanks for your ever welcome letter. Judging by the date it has been longer than usual on the road. It had been opened and the torn envelope stuck together again. It is possible however that it had been delivered to the wrong house and opened in error. You tell me you are sending Elena a 'fufaika'. Elena does not quite understand the word 'fufaika' but thinks that perhaps you mean 'sweater'. I have heard my mother mention the word 'fufaika'. On looking up my dictionary I see both words mean a 'knitted garment'. You would be surprised, Jenya, to know how many English and American words are creeping into our vocabulary but with a Russian emphasis and to the young are not foreign at all. Elena is looking forward to receiving your gift and sends her thanks. I have some news for you. The other night Seryozha called and informed us that we can expect to be grandparents in the early spring! This announcement called for a celebration and a glass or two of vodka! Seryozha and Elena have been married for seven years and we had given up hope of ever becoming grandparents. On the other hand we understood how difficult it is to have children when it is necessary for both parents to work. They are both qualified TV engineers and are employed in the broadcasting station in Leningrad. The other difficulty is accommodation. Originally after Seryozha and Elena were married they lived with us and used the spare bedroom. My Elena tried very hard to please them in every way but as our old proverb goes, 'No matter how much you feed a wolf he will still look to the woods'. After some months they left to live with Elena's mother. Of course we realised that to live with a mother-in-law is not the same as being with your own mother. The flat they share with young Elena's mother has only two rooms and conditions will be more cramped after the arrival of the baby, but that does not worry our young people. Seryozha has already bought the pram and cot. After all we Russians are quite hardened to living in conditions which I believe would not be tolerated in the West.

Elena's mother is younger and more able than my Elena to take care of the baby and allow her daughter to continue working. It is the universal practice here with all the babushkas playing an important part in our way of life.

We are are approaching November and as I write those lines it is snowing hard and covering everything with a thick white blanket – something I like to see.

We wish you and your family all the best in life.

Write! Please write!

Evgenie

January 1982

Dear Jenya,

Last week your parcel with the fufaika [sweater], tights and socks arrived safely. We are all delighted and Elena especially so with her fufaika which fits her very well. It is of such good quality and in her favourite shade of blue. We are ashamed we cannot send anything worth having in return. There are so many restrictions. The 'Berezka' shops which cater for tourists have a great variety of interesting articles, but we are not permitted to buy anything from them. Natasha, however, by some means managed to acquire one of these black lacquered boxes with a beautiful old Russian scene by Palek, but when she went to the Post Office she was not permitted to send it to you. Instead she has sent a string of amber beads and a box of chocolates, which she trusts will arrive safely.

Just now we are experiencing very unpleasant weather with a biting wind blowing from the Gulf of Finland. We do not go out for our usual walk and only leave the house to buy food and milk. I have been spending the time rearranging my album where I keep all the photographs you have sent me. I am admiring a picture of Michael taken on the deck of the ship when he first arrived in Bombay from Britain. He is dressed in his white uniform. How I envy him! He has seen more of the world in his four years at sea than I have during my sixteen years sailing, most of the time in fishing trawlers hundreds of miles from the shores in the Barents Sea or other northern waters. You have no idea how lonely and dark these waters can be. Here there is no place to hide during a snowstorm with the visibility nil and the wet snow clinging to the side of the ship, soon to freeze into a heavy mass of ice which threatens to overturn it. How good it was to be back to the bright lights of Murmansk! Throughout those years I continued to cherish the hope that one day I would sail on those distant seas and discover how the other half of the world lived. Sadly, no matter how often I applied for a place on a cargo ship and the necessary visa, the answer was a refusal – the reason being, I suspect, that I had relatives abroad.

One day, however, in the spring of 1941 I was offered the post of a senior engineer on a tramp steamer – a beautiful ship bought from Britain. There I had a spacious cabin and my own bathroom and there I joyfully settled down during the preparations for our departure, due on 23 June, for the distant East – Japan, China, Singapore etc., but while impatiently awaiting the promised visa, we received the dreadful news of Germany's sudden invasion of Russia. All my hopes vanished once more – I was directed instead to join a Soviet Navy ship. Our duty was to meet the convoys of British and Canadian ships bringing our supplies and to escort them to Murmansk. Terrible and frightening were the heroic journeys of these convoys paid for by a great loss of lives when skirting the dangerous shores of Norway where they were bombed from above and torpedoed from below. I myself was fished out of the Barents Sea – more dead than alive and taken to the hospital in Murmansk where I gradually recovered. Nearby was the hospital for our allies. I wanted very much to get to know them, but we were not allowed to fraternise and yet when meeting the British or American sailors at sea we always found them very friendly towards us and enjoyed talking to them as best as we could.

After my recovery, I was given the post of a 'spotter' aboard one of the ships. I, at that time, had very good eyesight and spent long hours on end searching the skies for enemy planes.

Just now as I am writing to you Seryozha has arrived. I will continue in my next letter and will ask Seryozha to post this one on his way home. We are always happy when members of our family call on us. Sadly that does not happen as often as we would like.

My Elena and Seryozha send their regards to you and all the family.

With love,
Evgenie

April 1983

Dear Jenya,

Thank you for your letter and photographs which arrived yesterday. They are as usual very interesting and much appreciated by us all. I have been arranging them in my album where I keep all pictures connected with Archangel. At times I like to imagine that we are sitting together and talking about old times and all our friends and relatives who are long since gone. Somehow I have never become quite used to living in this lovely city and keep hoping to pay another visit to old Archangel one of these days. I have to tell you that on 10 March Elena and I have been presented with a grandson. He is a sturdy child and weighed four kilos. He has been named Rodion but is referred to as Rodie. The family tell me that he bears a strong resemblance to me, but that perhaps is not so surprising as our Seryozha is the double of his grandfather – my father Aleksandr. Everything went very well and we are all very happy.

We have had another exciting event but of a different kind! Every year in Leningrad, an important dog-show takes place and our Natasha, who has a small silver grey poodle called Alice, decided to take her to the show which took place two days ago. In the morning my Elena and Natasha with 'Aliska' as we call her, set off for the dog-show. They arrived back in the early evening with Aliska proudly stepping in front with a gold medal tied round her neck.

To Elena's and Natasha's delighted surprise, Aliska had won the prize for the best dog in the show. Sadly, however, Natasha has decided to part with Aliska in a few months and pass her over to us, the reason being that Natasha is expecting to become a mother in October and feels she could not cope with Aliska and a baby. Elena and I are a bit concerned as Natasha is now in her early thirties and that is not the best time to have her first child. She has retired meantime from the stage and we can only hope that all will go well. Natasha's father-in-law owns a cottage in the country, where he grows vegetables and berries and Natasha and her husband, also named Jenya, are planning to spend July there. Leningrad becomes hot and stuffy at times and those who are fortunate to have a cottage in the country like to live there during the summer. Seryozha has hired a cottage in a village near the Gulf of Finland and young Elena and Rodie plan to spend two months there. Seryozha has to attend to his work but hopes to spend his weekends and the odd week or two with Elena and his son.

My Elena and I will be content to take our usual stroll accompanied by our cat Yashka. I am just wondering how he and Aliska will get along together! I have no other news and will close meanwhile.

Elena and I send our love and best wishes to you all. I kiss and embrace you.

Evgenie

July 1983

Dear Jenya,

Your welcome letter of 21st June arrived three days ago. It has taken a month to cross the skies from Scotland! The following day we received the parcel with the suit for Rodion. We are all delighted with it. Such a lovely article would be quite impossible to find here. At present it is too large, but will fit Rodie perfectly next summer. Seryozha and Elena are very grateful for such a handsome gift. You are asking me if there might be a christening. I have to tell you that our son and daughter know nothing at all about religion. They never had it at school, nor were they ever encouraged to attend church. Yet I have to admit that nowadays many parents are having their children baptised. There are also cases of adults deciding to be christened. In their case the priest will say a prayer and sprinkle a few drops of water over their heads. The spreading of religion is also seen in cemeteries where the simple stones are being removed and replaced by crosses as was the old custom in the Orthodox Church.

Incidentally, I always believed that I was christened in our local church of the Assumption, but now you tell me the baptism took place at home. Elena and I were very amused when reading your description of what followed. I never knew that my young godfather, Yura, had declined to stay for the celebration and had left for home, saying he had an important essay to write, but Babushka, suspecting that her young Yurochka was lying, decided to follow him and on arriving found him in bed with the young maid Marietta!! I can almost see our babushka with towel in hand chasing that girl out of the house and how later you found Babushka sitting on the edge of the bed weeping bitterly and my young godfather on his knees, swearing he would never do it again. I can understand how you, only eight years old, were bewildered by all the fuss – Dedushka administering Valerian drops to soothe Babushka's nerves while Kapochka patted her hands, and all because two people decided to have a little rest together! I have to admit that my young uncle was always more adventurous than his more sedate brother Seryozha and it is sad to realise that none of them ever reached old age.

Aliska has arrived – complete with bed, lead, dish and a long list of instructions which we have chosen to ignore. She is a friendly little thing but the problem is with Yashka who is madly jealous and cannot stand this interloper whose friendly overtures are met with the threatening growling of a tiger – all set to tear her apart! We fear for Aliska's eyes and have been forced to keep our 'lodgers' in separate rooms. The day when we can return Aliska cannot come quick enough. Meanwhile we still enjoy our walks with Aliska on her lead and Yashka in his own way of appearing and vanishing to be eventually found sitting on the steps awaiting our arrival.

We are very anxious as Natasha's time draws near. She is not keeping well but we have a very good clinic here and she is getting the best of attention. We can but hope that all will go well with our daughter.

Just now we are experiencing very hot weather – the door to our balcony is wide open and I can see the flowers in full bloom in their boxes. Our local stores are selling berries – raspberries, strawberries and fruit of every description. They are even selling wild strawberries which are delicious. Elena is kept busy making jam.

It is time for me to stop. We send our love to you all. I kiss and embrace you.

Write please write!

Evgenie

November 1983

Dear Jenya,

Your welcome letter of 12 September we received on 4 October, the day our Natasha was taken to hospital for the birth of her baby. Please excuse the delay with my answer. We have been through a very anxious time, as the birth proved to be extremely difficult and there were times when we wondered whether, in spite of the excellent attention from the doctors and nurses, our daughter would survive her travail.

On 15 October our grandson was born. He was a smally baby and a week later developed jaundice, however both mother and son have recovered and as I write are back are in their home. Our grandson has been named Alexsandr, after his great-grandfather, my father. He will probably be referred to as Shurick, or Sanya, Sasha, or Alick, for as you know the Aleksandr has many diminutives.

I am sitting alone writing to you with only Yashka and Aliska for company. Elena is away to Natasha's house to help her with the baby. It is a journey of two hours as Natasha and Jenya live at the other end of Leningrad. Their small flat of two rooms is on the eighth floor of a high building. There is a small balcony, where Natasha plans to keep the pram from which the baby can watch the birds flying past and have the benefit of being in the fresh air.

It has turned very cold. Everything is covered by a thick mantle of snow. The heavy-laden branches of the birches are sparkling in the sun and the scenery is that of a Christmas card! With Elena being away all day, I have been occupying myself attending to our windows. We have double glazing but each autumn they require attention to keep out all the draughts. I wonder if you also require double glazing?

Elena has just arrived. She tells me that the baby is doing well. He is now almost four kilos, loves his bath and is beginning to notice the strange world around him. Elena does not think that she will require to go back as Natasha is managing very well and the journey is very tiring for Elena. We both send our regards and best wishes to you and Ron, to George and Michael and all the others.

I embrace and kiss you. Please write!

Evgenie

———————————

January 1984

Dear Jenya,

Many thanks for your letter of 9 December with the enclosed Christmas cards. Your letters are always a source of great pleasure and I enjoy reading them over and over again. This one has taken exactly a month to travel, but everything was in order. The parcel with the knitted jacket and cap for Alick also arrived safely, Natasha is delighted with them and asks me to convey her grateful thanks to Ron's sister for her beautiful work.

Natasha wishes she could write her appreciation in English, but sadly she does not know English although she is quite fluent in German. Her group have several times performed in East Germany but her greatest ambition is to travel to other parts of the world.

Meanwhile she is very occupied looking after her baby. Alick is a good-natured child always ready to smile!

You ask me if there has been a christening party. I do not remember if I mentioned before that our children are not religious and have never been taught religion at school. I myself can be described as being half religious and something of what my babushka taught me has remained with me. My Elena is more religious and occasionally goes to church. I at times accompany her and light a candle and somehow in the flickering light I seem to see again the faces of all those who at one time were a part of my existence.

Elena and I were very interested to read about the journey with your boys from Bombay to Scotland in 1944 for the purpose of starting their education. From all accounts you were sailing over dangerous waters with the Japanese submarines lurking in the Indian Ocean. It was a risky journey to undertake; you were lucky to have made it. I at that time was likewise at sea and was twice fished out of the Barents Sea, something from which I have never quite recovered. Through the whole of the war while serving in our fleet I never knew anything about the fate of my mother, brother and sisters. To all my letters there were no replies and there were times when I believed I was the sole survivor. In 1945, the ship on which I served was in Germany and there to my great joy I received a letter from Victoria. In 1946 I was demobbed and arrived in Leningrad where I met my mother, who, with my stepsister Nora, had been repatriated from Germany. Vika also arrived from the east of Russia to where she had been evacuated and had worked in a children's home. My brother Shurick was in Moscow – likewise later demobbed, but we knew nothing about Olga until two years later when, to our surprise, we received a letter from her in America.

To this day we do not know how she landed there. These first days in Leningrad were terribly difficult. Money meant nothing. We had no spare clothing nor even the barest necessities of life and nowhere to live. Fortunately Victoria was able to reclaim her old room in Ulitza Marata, where she settled with husband and family and took my mother and Nora as well.

I was lucky enough to find a small room near the Moscow Station. We all started from scratch, but gradually our lives began to improve. I will stop meanwhile. We are expecting Vika and her husband to call this evening and no doubt we shall sit and talk the whole night through about these distant days and all the hardships we endured.

Elena sends her regards to you and your family.

I await your next letter and kiss and embrace you,

Evgenie

Author's note

At this point it has to be said that until the fall of communism it would have been dangerous for cousin Olga to describe to her brother the circumstances which took her to America for there was always the possibility of the letter being opened and involving Evgenie in interrogation by the K.G.B. I happen to know of the events which led to Olga being in America, but to describe them I have to go back to the year 1946 when I, with my husband, was living in India.

One day to my astonishment I received a letter which had been sent from Germany to my home address in Dundee and forwarded to India. It was from cousin Olga who was safe and well and living in a camp in the American zone. Sadly, beyond sending parcels, I was not in a position to offer hospitality in India and by the time we returned to Scotland, Olga and the young man she married were in America and doing well for themselves.

From that first letter received in India long years ago and up till now our correspondence continued and it is through this exchange of letters and Olga's short visit to Scotland that I learned about all the events that took place in the aftermath of the war which were as follows:

At the start of the war, Olga, with her mother and stepsister Nora, were living in Ukraina, after spending some years in the wild depths of Siberia where Victor, Aunt Shura's second husband, was serving a sentence of exile for having fought as an officer in the White Army against the communists.

On their return from Siberia they were permitted to live in the Ukraine where Victor owned a cottage occupied by his mother. There they happily settled down but, sadly, one day during Stalin's frightening thirties the police arrived, took Victor away and shot him. The family were told never to ask any questions. With the start of the second war, Germany soon occupied the Ukraine including the village where lived Olga and family. I recall Olga telling me: 'My sister Nora and I were first hidden in the cellar but later when we emerged they did not treat us too badly. They took some fruit, eggs and a hen or two. It was worse in other parts and we considered ourselves to be comparatively lucky. Later, when the Russian army was advancing and the Germans retreating, we and many of the civilians, afraid of persecution or whatever from our own soldiers, likewise went to Germany where we were given armlets and treated as slave labour.

'We rejoiced when the war was won and our soldiers marched into Germany. Now, we thought we would go back and start afresh, but instead we were being rounded up and sent to Russia to stand trial for our so-called treachery. My mother, with Nora, was sent to the north of Russia where she suffered great hardship but after a year was allowed to go to Leningrad where she met Jenya and Vika. I was likewise arrested and taken to the barracks now occupied by the Russian troops where, suspected of spying or God only knows what, I was placed in solitary confinement and questioned night and day until I thought I would lose my reason and begged them to shoot me. I was there in that filthy cell just as I stood with no change of clothing and feeling utterly degraded. Perhaps the only brightness to sustain me was from a young soldier on watch who at times would look through the peephole in the door and say, "Never mind, kitten, when this is over I'll marry you and take you back with me to Ukraina".

'On the fourth day, an important general arrived who became infuriated when he discovered what was being done to me. I was immediately freed and allowed to wash and tidy myself. Later he informed me that I would be taken to join a group of other Russians due to be sent to Russia for interrogation. "If you are innocent," he said, "you will be freed – if guilty punished."

'A week later a group of fellow Russians and I, all under guard, were standing in the station waiting for the train to take us back to Russia. All were silent, all were tense. None of us were spies, we loved our land – but what did she hold for us? Just then I was suddenly overcome by an urgent need to use the toilet. I approached our guard and explained my predicament and he kindly offered to escort me to the waiting room at the other end of the station where I thankfully dived in, leaving him on guard outside.

'When I came out he was standing a few yards away with his back to me chatting up a young German fraulein. Some yards away to the right was a wired fence behind which stood a train that appeared to be on the point of leaving for the West. This, I realised, was a heaven-sent opportunity. Running as fast as my legs could carry me, I reached the fence, climbed over, tearing my leg in the process, jumped on the train, opened the door of a compartment and fell in just as the train began to move!

'Inside was a young schoolboy, a friendly, kind boy, who bandaged my bleeding leg with his handkerchief. It transpired he was on his way to visit his grandmother. We travelled together for some hours until we reached a small town, where we both got off. He, knowing the town, escorted me to a hospital where he left me and went off to his grandmother. I never saw again my kind young saviour.

'The staff in the hospital were helpful and there again I was lucky, for after bandaging my leg and having a friendly talk, they suggested I should stay on as they were short of staff and I could work there – an offer which I gratefully accepted. The hospital was a wonderful refuge with the doctors and nurses being very kind to me, but in the end, after some weeks fearing that there was a possibility of being caught up by the Russians, I moved further west.

'It is a long story, but I eventually landed in a refugee camp under American supervision. There I met a young man – Victor Arnautow, whom I married.

Some time later we were allowed to leave for America where Vitya's parents were already resident along with some of our friends. We settled down in New York.

'At first life was hard. We worked in a restaurant serving and washing dishes, but gradually everything improved. Vitya was a civil engineer and succeeded in finding a good job. I learned the language and worked in an office. We made good money, rented a small flat in pleasant surroundings and settled down to enjoy life in America.

March 1984

Dear Jenya,

Your long-awaited letter arrived yesterday morning. I am hastening to tell you that I fully understand the reason for the delay, and how delighted I am to know that you have succeeded in finishing your book and have been kept busy going over all that you have written. I have to admit it is a little sad for me to realise that it has been written in English, a language I do not know, but do not be sorry on my account for throughout the past years you have told me so much about all the events that took place in our family of which I was unaware, that I feel I am well acquainted with the contents of your book. I congratulate you my dear Jenya and hope with all my heart that it will be published and that many people will read and enjoy it.

I note you have decided to call it *The House by the Dvina*. Yes, that is a good name. It was a warm, hospitable house with a garden like something out of a fairy tale. I am glad that for a short time I also knew it.

You ask me, Jenya, what made me leave the sea for work ashore. It is a sad question I sometimes ask myself. Sixteen years at sea is after all a short space of time for one who had dreamt and planned to go to sea from the days he sat behind a school desk. It so happened that after being discharged from the navy, I decided to apply for a visa which would allow me to find a place on a ship that could take me across the warm seas to those distant tropical shores of which I had read and dreamt of so much and longed to see.

I saw no reason for any refusal. After all I had been promised I would be granted a visa shortly before the start of the war and was actually aboard the ship, all set to sail, when the sudden attack by Germany cancelled all plans. I was transferred to the navy, in which I served throughout the whole of the war and was twice miraculously fished out of the icy waters of the Barents Sea. With all these credits on my side I submitted my application to the powers that be and full of hope awaited a favourable reply.

Some three weeks later after spending the evening with Victoria and her family I found the long awaited letter in my postbox. I sat down at the table and with trembling fingers opened the envelope. The reply was brief and to the point. There was no possibility of granting me the visa, but at the same time they were prepared to offer me a position as a qualified engineer, on a ship sailing to the Baltic ports. For some moments I sat wondering why was it that they could not grant me this longed-for visa when a friend with less experience and qualification was sailing somewhere to the tropical East and why was it that I had to be contained in that Baltic 'pond'?

Suddenly I realised the reason was my German surname of Scholts passed on to me from some distant ancestor about whom we knew nothing at all. It was for that same reason and his connections with Finland and relatives abroad that my father was denied all work. Now this curt response to my letter had destroyed all the dreams and hopes I had cherished throughout my whole life. Outraged by such injustice I stood up, crumpled the offending letter, threw it to the floor and, unable to contain my anger, rushed out of the house.

I walked the whole night through along the empty streets, not knowing or caring where I was going and in the morning returned to the house. Exhausted, I threw myself on my bed and fell into a deep sleep. On awakening in the late afternoon, I rose, picked up the crumpled letter and read again the contents. I then sat down at the table and wrote to the authorities telling them that I had decided to leave the sea and would try to find some work ashore. About a week later I was offered a position as an engineer in one of our factories. So ended my sailing days of sixteen years and all my cherished dreams.

You may well ask me did I not regret this hasty decision? I admit that at times there were regrets and especially considering that if I had remained at sea I would have been entitled to a larger pension than the one that comes to me now.

I have found, however, that there are compensations. I met Elena and we have led a happy life together. At first things were difficult. We were both working and bringing up our children in one room, but gradually our way of life improved. The children did well at school and later Natasha attended the Art College and Sergei the University. He has a good position in the Leningrad TV and his wife Elena is also employed there.

Natasha is a very talented actress and has travelled with her group all over Russia and abroad as far as East Germany, Czechoslovakia, Finland and the Baltic States. Her great ambition is to visit Britain and France, but as she is now in her thirties I doubt if she will ever be granted her wish. Elena and I have often wondered from whom she inherited this talent. It is certainly not from her parents.

Do you remember Uncle Adya who was our fathers' cousin? He was known to be a very talented young man and after the family timber business was confiscated, Adya and his wife Nataliya became professional actors and performed in Leningrad and all over Russia. Sadly, in the early Thirties, Adya was arrested and sent to Siberia where he probably perished. His wife, likewise, died but one day, when walking on Nevsky Prospect, I met their son, Shurick, who told me he was also on the stage and making a good living from it which I was very pleased to hear.

Elena and I are grateful that our son and daughter have done quite well for themselves. We do not see them as often as we would like, but that is the way of life. There is a touch of spring in the air and Elena is already working in our little garden on the balcony. The seeds of the little 'strangers' which you sent two years ago have taken again.

Elena sends her love.

Write! Please write!

Evgenie

May 1984

Dear Jenya,

Many thanks for your letter of 19 April. I am pleased to note that George has handed in a copy to each of the two publishers in Edinburgh. Elena and I send you our best wishes and hopes for this book to come out into the world and that those who will buy it will enjoy reading about all the events that took place in our family. It would be lovely if the book could reach us also, but that would be impossible as I have been told no foreign literature is allowed to enter Russia.

You are asking me where exactly did Dedushka and Babushka spend their exile. It was in a village called Emetsk which is situated on the shores of the Dvina some fifty miles to the south of Archangel. It is a beautiful place with lakes, woods and a little river running through it. It is my belief that they liked living there. The people were kind and in return for Dedushka's attention to them used to bring butter, milk and berries in the summer. It was a better life than in Archangel where Dedushka had to attend the hospital at the other end of the town, at times having to walk there in the dead of winter. In the house which they shared with other people they also suffered endless persecution from that horrible 'Chechenka' woman, who, as I described before, was the cause of Babushka's death. They might have wished to go on living in Emetsk had it not been that they missed the family. Of course they were terribly upset to hear about the fire in the house with the awful destruction and loss of their belongings and the vandalising of the garden.

On their return to Archangel Babushka never went near the house or the street and just lived with memories until she died. In the summer of 1929 they returned to Emetsk and took me with them. I can still see Dedushka sitting peacefully beside the river with a fishing rod in his hand and Babushka nearby, engaged in her knitting. It was the time of the *'goloobitsa'*. Do you remember, Jenya, that lovely blue-coloured berry which is larger and sweeter than the *'chernika'* [blackberry] which appears later and is more tedious to pick? I spent my days in the woods gathering *goloobitsa*, picking mushrooms and often swimming in the warm waters of the Dvina.

We were staying in the cottage of a friendly peasant and his wife who fed us with buckwheat kasha and fish soup made from fish caught in the river. I was fourteen at the time and these two weeks in Emetsk are for ever etched in my memory as the happiest days of my youth. We returned to Archangel carrying baskets filled with *goloobitsa* and mushrooms which we shared with Marga and the children.

Our grandsons are keeping well. Rodie is now walking and Alick is smiling and waving his hands as if he would like to say something. Next month they all will be leaving for the country. Vicka has already left for her cottage.

Leningrad as you know was built on marshy ground and many citizens (especially the mothers!) believe the air in the summer is bad for the children. Elena and I shall content ourselves with our daily walks accompanied by Aliska and Yashka. Nearby is a beautiful lake where hundreds of wild ducks and various other birds like to congregate. Lots of people visit the lake to enjoy watching and feeding the birds and no one would dream of hurting them. In the autumn, when there is a touch of frost in the air, all these wild ducks gather together and prepare for their flight to warmer climes. I once counted three hundred wild ducks, but actually there were more of them. The drakes are particularly lovely. We enjoy living here in spite of it being some considerable distance from the centre of the town.

I am sending you a small book about the Scottish architect Cameron and all that he created during the reign of Catherine II. I think it may interest you. I kiss and embrace you – Elena sends her love.

Write!

Yours,

Evgenie

—————

August 1984

Dear Jenya,

There is no sign as yet in the postbox of the familar envelope, but hopefully it may arrive one of these days. I realise of course that you lead a far busier life than I do and now perhaps will be occupied with your book.

I wonder if your publishers are printing in it some of the old photographs? They would I think greatly enhance the book as the copies of the ones you sent me are very interesting. I was so glad to receive them and keep them carefully arranged in a separate album. We have had a lovely summer but now it is drawing to a close.

The shops are full of every kind of berry. There is also a variety of fruit – melons, peaches, grapes etc., which have all arrived from the south. I have not been keeping too well of late and recently, when I was walking back to the house with a bottle of milk, as I do every morning, suddenly to my surprise the bottle fell from my hand which for some reason became lifeless and hung loosely by my side. I picked up the bottle which was fortunately plastic and put my useless left hand in my pocket. I must admit the thought that I may have lost the use of my arm for good frightened me but as I continued walking it seemed as if life was slowly returning to it and by the time I reached the house my arm was normal.

We have a very good clinic nearby which I have been attending for treatment to my eyes as my eyesight is getting weaker and affecting my writing, something perhaps you have noticed. There I was also given pills which have to be taken each day for my general health. I have had a rather hard life in the past and perhaps am paying for it now.

Last week Shurick arrived from Moscow. He spent the night with us and in the morning left for Vika's cottage where he intends to help her with some repairs to the roof of her cottage. My brother is a very life-loving, cheerful man in spite of having suffered more than the rest of us. He fought throughout the whole of the war but towards the end was caught and imprisoned by the Germans. After two unsuccessful attempts to escape he was transferred to a camp where they were conducting experiments on prisoners. Twice, Shurick was immersed in freezing cold water to find out the lowest temperature a man could experience and survive and would probably have perished had he been subjected to another test, but was saved by the Russian Army advancing and overrunning the camp. After the war he was discharged in Moscow and later married a war widow with one child and now has a daughter and son of his own.

He works for the government as a builder and as his wife likewise works, they have a comfortable income between them. In spite of being scattered like dried leaves in the wind, we four have always tried to keep in touch with each other. I was the lucky one living with our babushka. My mother, with Olga, followed her second husband exiled to Siberia and later to Ukraina. Shurick was left with a friend in Archangel and Vika, eleven years old, was sent by train to Leningrad to live with Cousin Irina (Aunt Olga's daughter) and her husband, Baron Peter Brock. He was at one time a colonel in the Semeynovski Regiment and was spared until the late Thirties when he and a few fellow officers were executed by Stalin.

Prior to this tragedy, so many people during the Twenties lived in Brock's house. Uncle Sereyzha with his wife and two children stayed there and even Kapochka, who once lived with Babushka and later with us, joined the throng. Peter's wife (Cousin Irina) left the house with her little daughter, to stay for some time with her mother (Aunt Olga) but somehow never returned.

Vika, although foisted on relatives she hardly knew, faced up bravely to her embarrassing situation, worked hard to please and, having learned to drive, acted as a driver to various people – including some important commissars. Later she met and married a young man who was a staunch communist. There is something very strong and undaunted in my sister's character. She and her husband are devoted to each other, but it is Vika who plans and organises everything and it was Vika who decided to build a cottage in the country and worked very hard to gather the money. We three keep in constant touch with each other, but sadly, although our little sister Olga writes to us all, we do not think she will ever return to Russia.

I must stop now. Elena and I are planning to go into town and visit Natasha. I shall post this letter from the main post office as it is more reliable than those outside the town. I shall go on hoping to see soon the familiar envelope.

Elena sends her best wishes. I embrace and kiss you.

Evgenie

November, 1984

Dear Jenya,

I was so glad to receive your letter of 3 November and fully understand the delay. Elena and I are delighted to know that your book is now launched into the world and send you our heartiest congratulations. We note that you have to go to London where the interviews you gave were broadcast. How wonderful it all must have been.

It is good that Michael is at present in London and was able to meet you and put you up in his flat. Although we realise that at present we cannot receive a copy, I have a strong feeling that one day your book will reach us. I think it is important that our children should know all that took place in those distant days, and perhaps not only just our children but other people as well. My mother used to recall certain events, but she knew very little about what happened long ago and I have learned more from you passing on Babushka's recollections to which she rarely referred when we were living together, being very much afraid of the Chechenka woman hovering around.

It is sad that Babushka and especially Uncle Gherman are not here to know of your achievements. They would have been so proud and so would Archangel be if the book should ever reach it.

I forgot to mention in my last letter to you that when Shurick called the last time, he suggested we should both take a trip to Archangel this next summer, and put the graves of our relatives in order, but as my health is not so good these days Elena will not hear of my going there. The last visit I paid to Archangel was in 1964 when my mother and I went together. We saw a lot of changes and the most exciting experience of all was when we reached the Station of Issaka-gorka on the west bank and the train continued thundering across the river on a mighty bridge, straight into the centre of the town. Gone were the days when to reach the town, we had to cross either by boat during the summer, or horse and sledge in the winter.

The Dvina in bygone days was known to provide the best possible transport for goods. At times freezing to a depth of almost a metre, it carried several horse-drawn caravans all moving together to the south. That wonderful sight is seen no more. In fact I saw no horses at all except on one occasion when, coming out of the cemetery, I met a single horse walking slowly with bowed head and dragging a cart with a coffin on top. An old, sad-looking man was walking beside it. I stood, also overcome by sadness, watching them gradually vanish inside.

We spent two weeks in Archangel with Aunt Nastya and Uncle Andrei. The weather was warm and sunny and each day I enjoyed swimming in the soft waters of the Dvina, something I had not done for years. Our main purpose was to tend to the graves. Both Mother and I worked hard clearing the weeds and having the crosses repaired and painted. The granite monuments were standing up to the ravages of time except the one to our grandfather which, whether due to the weather or vandalism, was lying in two pieces. The plaques which had been laid in front of each monument had all been stolen, which was a pity as on them were etched the names of those other relatives who had died and were buried somewhere abroad. After the work in the cemetery was finished we set off to visit Babushka's house.

The last time I was there the gates were locked but now they were standing wide open. We timidly walked in. To the right, where at one time were rows of frames used for growing cucumbers and a hot-house for forcing tomatoes and rare flowers, was now a mass of broken glass and rusty pieces of iron. Further along, where once stood the stables and the coach-house, there was nothing bar a heap of rubbish and even the lodge which used to overlook the garden was likewise gone.

The house, however, although grey and shoddy, still appeared to be in order. A woman who had been watching us from an open window called out, 'What do you want?'

'My Babushka once lived here,' I replied.

'You can't come in,' she rejoined. 'There are no floors; they have all been used for firewood. I'm the caretaker here and live alone in one small room, but if you care you can take a walk in what is left of the garden.'

The pond was the only thing that was left of the garden. There were no lawns, no trees, no hedge, no bushes and not a single flower. Mother and I spent some time sitting beside the pond. The two white jetties and the summer house on the west side, where Dedushka kept his beehives in the winter, were no more. There was a silence and a deep sadness hanging over the whole place.

Do you remember that other summer house that looked like something out of a fairy tale? Do you remember the fun we had when peering through the coloured panes, seeing the garden in all the different hues? There is no trace of it now – the little hill is covered by weeds of every description.

We wandered aimlessly for a little while and prior to leaving I took a picture of Mother sitting beside the pond, a copy of which I will enclose in this letter. Beyond my mother's relatives we met no one whom we knew. All have vanished somewhere. Youra's son Alecksei, with his wife and family, were somewhere in the south, although I heard recently that they have returned to Archangel.

There were of course a lot of changes and many strange faces, but we were glad to note that the lovely avenue of birches on the river front and the river itself are still the same.

As I write just now I am reminded of a strange coincidence which took place in the summer of 1972 when our Natasha and her troupe were sent to perform in Archangel. One day, having asked permission to go for a stroll on her own, she decided to walk beside the river. As she continued on her way, having in mind the description of the house and carefully scanning each building, she suddenly came upon it standing on the corner of the river front and Ulitza Gaidara. It was shabby and grey with broken windows but still whole – and she stood beside it remembering all that she had heard about the people who at one time lived there.

Then she noticed a bulldozer moving along the street and coming up close to the house. She watched in total disbelief as in a short space of time, the house about which she had heard so much was reduced to a heap of rubble. It was an amazing and sad coincidence that the final destruction of the house built by our grandfather, Aleksandr Scholts, would be witnessed by his great-granddaughter Natasha. I can almost hear our Babushka saying 'Strange are the ways of our Lord'.

And now my dear Jenya, I think I have come to the end of a very long letter which I trust will not tire you too much when translating it to Ronald.

Elena sends her love. I look forward to your letter and all your news.

I kiss and embrace you,

Evgenie

January 1985

Dear Jenya,

Thank you very much for the lovely Christmas card, the Fraser tartan scarf, tights for Elena and the girls and the sweaters for our grandsons. I am especially delighted to receive the Fraser scarf and shall wear it with great pleasure. We are glad to note in the enclosed letter that the perfume, chocolates, and the little lacquer box arrived safely.

You are enquiring what duty we might have had to pay. We paid five roubles which according to our papers is £5 – in short, one rouble being equal to £1. I am not certain if in reality this is quite correct.

I was very interested to read that in November when you were due to give a talk on the television about your book, this talk had to be cut short as someone, an expert on Russian affairs, was coming on instead to say a few words about our Michael Gorbachev who had been staying in Edinburgh but had to cut short his visit and return to Moscow. Although Elena and I rarely discuss politics we have heard it said that he is the coming man.

We are having the usual January weather of bitter winds and snows. Elena is away visiting Natasha and I am alone with Yashka and Aliska. They get along together not too badly, although at times when Aliska becomes too bothersome, the cat retaliates by inflicting severe scratches. We have had to cut his claws, an operation which raised loud protests, but at the present moment he is sitting at peace close to Aliska.

I am also at peace putting the finishing touches to a model of the ship *Gostorg* which went down close to the rocky coast of Novaya Zemlya, an event which I described to you some time ago. Modelling ships is my favourite hobby and before *Gostorg* I made a model of an old sailing ship which had been built in Archangel during the time of Peter the Great.

This work demands good eyesight which sadly I no longer have as you may have noticed by my writing. I have been informed by the clinic that there is no cure as it is due to the hardening of the arteries and as time goes on my eyesight will get worse, something to which I'm not looking forward.

Our postwoman who, at times, likes to deliver letters personally, has just handed in a letter from Olga. We have not heard from her for some time and were beginning to get anxious. I was glad to note that all is well and delighted to learn that my little sister is actually planning to visit you in the summer. I am a little anxious about this long flight from America to Scotland, but at the same time glad for her for, although she never says so, I feel she must be lonely at times especially since she lost her husband, and this visit to you will be a glorious experience for her.

I must stop. I promised Elena I would prepare our evening meal.

I embrace and kiss you. My regards to Ron and once again many thanks for everything.

Evgenie

March 1985

Dear Jenya,

Your welcome letter of 27 January arrived on 26 February and thus has taken almost a month to reach here by airmail. There is no accounting for such a delay but I am glad to know that all is well with you and the family. Here we have had a cold and snowy winter accompanied by winds blowing from the Gulf of Finland. Now there is a faint touch of spring in the air with the promise of better days to come.

Our grandsons are growing. Both are walking. The elder one speaks quite well, the younger chatters in a language of his own and likes to sing to himself. I have been thinking, Jenya, how lovely it would be if you and Ron could visit us. Things are different now and it would be quite possible for you to stay with us. We have a spare room which I use as my work room but it could be easily turned into a bedroom which it was when Sergei and Elena lived for some time with us after their marriage. Please think about it. It would be so wonderful if after these long years I could meet you again.

You ask me if I have received the picture of Petya, our late cousin Jenya's son with whom you were staying in Paris last summer. I am sorry to say that letter and picture have not arrived and must have gone astray somewhere. It is sad that Cousin Jenya died so young, as did most of her sisters in Finland including Marina, the only one I knew out of those eight girls. Vika, of course, knew Irina, the wife of Peter Brock, as she lived with them until Peter was executed along with his brother officers during the terrible reign of Stalin. This would never have happened nowadays as, thank God, things have changed for the better.

I am anxiously waiting for a letter from Olga, as I would like to know on what date she plans to fly to Scotland. I have no other news. Elena and I lead a quiet life with nothing unusual ever happening to us. Your letters are always a great treat to us.

I kiss and embrace you and send my regards to Ron and all the members of the family including my cousin Alistair and Nora. I trust all is well with him and his family. Elena sends her love.

Evgenie

May 1985

Dear Jenya,

Thank you for your welcome letter of 18 April which I received the other day. I am glad to read that all is well with you and the family. I note that you have received a letter from Olga in which she is advising you that she will be arriving in Scotland on 30 May, in which case this letter should reach you while she is still with you and I would thank you to pass on our love and tell her that we will be thinking about this wonderful meeting.

You know Jenya, it is difficult to imagine Olga as the little girl who sat on our uncle's bed clutching her doll and listening to his stories, not quite understanding what it was all about, and would later spend her childhood in the depth of the Siberian Taiga, from there to Ukraina, then on to Germany, America and now to Scotland. 'How strange are the ways of our Lord!'

Here spring is back, the trees are green and the days growing longer. Our little Lemon Tree is twenty-two years old today. It is again covered in masses of lovely white blossoms with the sweet scent wafting through our room. Elena is back to her favourite ploy on the balcony planting seeds of her favourite flowers, including what we refer to as 'strangers', the seeds of which she had collected from the pretty blue flowers grown originally from a packet of seeds you sent two years ago.

I forgot to mention in my last letter that recently there was another important dog show held in Leningrad to which Elena and I decided to take our Aliska. We set off for the show and on arriving Elena with Aliska walked round and showed her in the ring as required by the judges. To our great delight and pride Aliska once again received the gold medal. Aliska is described as a 'blue miniature poodle' and when the sun shines on her coat, it takes on a pure shade of blue. Elena would like Aliska to have pups which could be sold and bring us some money but as Aliska came from France it would be difficult to find a dog of a similar breed here. In any case I am against having more dogs in the house. We have had enough trouble between Yashka and Aliska without asking for more.

On 1 May there were the usual celebrations in Leningrad with marches, bands playing and masses of onlookers. Having seen it all before I was not in the mood to join in but instead, following Elena's advice to visit Rodion and show him all my medals, set off to Seryozha's flat. Incidentally I do not think that my medals are for some acts of bravery as all soldiers and sailors who fought in the war received medals similar to mine.

I spent a happy hour or two with my grandson perched on my knees, playing with the medals and asking many questions. He is a very bright child and speaks quite fluently for one so young. Seryozha, his wife and son and his mother-in-law live in a one-room flat plus the usual kitchen and bathroom etc., but Seryozha is not alone in this as it is very difficult to find a flat to his taste and yet be near his place of business.

Leningrad is very overcrowded. We are lucky to have a spacious flat, but that is because we live outside the town along with many people who are retired and others who do not mind the long journey into the city centre. Our building was built after the war, but there are new houses springing up and more people arriving. Elena and I enjoy living in our roomy flat – at one time we were living in very cramped and horrible conditions – but as it is often said, 'We Russians are accustomed to suffering'.

I keep thinking about Olga's flight across the Atlantic and am anxiously awaiting your reply. I dislike flying and would rather cross a stormy sea in a ship than be confined inside a plane. I must stop meanwhile.

I kiss and embrace you. Elena sends her love.

Yours,

Evgenie

Author's Note

In the early morning of 1 June 1985 my son George and I set off for Prestwick Airport to meet my cousin Olga, due to arrive there from New York. We watched the aeroplane land and the passengers starting to disembark then hurried down to the reception hall. It was decided that while I stood at one entrance into the hall, my son would watch the other. There was a certain anxiety that we might miss her, for although we had corresponded for almost forty years, we had never met before and there had been no exchange of photographs beyond a small picture taken with her husband shortly after their arrival in America. As I stood watching the last of the passengers pouring out and seeing no one whom I imagined could be Olga, I became alarmed but, glancing across to Geroge, was relieved to see a small woman approaching him. It transpired that Olga was one of the last passengers to leave the aircraft and, although there were crowds of people in the hall, she unerringly went up to George and with a light American accent enquired 'Are you by any chance George Fraser?' and on hearing that he was, threw her arms around him! Back in Edinburgh there was the meeting with Ronald followed by lunch and thus began my cousin's holiday in Scotland.

The twelve days' leave she had been granted by her office were not enough for such a special visit and sadly passed too quickly. Ronald took her to the Castle and other places of interest. There was a tour by bus around Edinburgh, including a visit to Holyrood Palace – a place of special interest to Olga as she had been taught in school about the life and fate of Mary, Queen of Scots. There were, of course, meetings with friends and relatives and my brother with his wife, Nora, threw a large party to which all the relatives and friends were invited.

Olga in turn, like all Russians, brought gifts for everyone, forgetting no one. Before our meeting I at times wondered what kind of a person was my cousin. On getting to know her I discovered she was blessed with a very calm nature, one not easily ruffled, and also, in spite of the suffering she endured, found she was deeply religious and when relating more details of her amazing escape to the American zone, she firmly maintained it was God who saved her. At the same time, like some of our Russian relations, she is not short of humour. Talking about her work in the office in charge of several young girls, Olga could be extremely funny when describing in her American/Russian accent all their antics and especially the conversations on the telephone with their boyfriends.

Michael, eager to meet Olga, invited both of us to spend some days in the delightful village of Chew Magna, near Bristol, where he lived with his wife Jennifer and family. We spent four days there being driven around the lovely English countryside – a rare experience for Olga – and in between times sitting in the garden watching the children playing, meeting neighbours who were curious about Russia and liked to hear about our experiences – so different from their own well-regulated lives. It was there that she and I together sent a postcard to Evgenie in the hope that it might reach Leningrad.

The days passed all too quickly and when leaving it was decided that we would go back to Edinburgh by bus and in this way Olga would see more of England and Scotland than she would have if we travelled by train. That turned out to be a mistake. The journey was too long and tiresome and not helped by the accompaniment of loud, tuneless music on the radio which continued until nearing Scotland where it ceased after some of the passengers objected to it. It was a relief to be back in Edinburgh, but sadly only two days remained before she was due to return to America.

We spent the time reminiscing over the past. I recollect asking Olga if she planned to take a trip to Leningrad to meet the family. 'Not meantime but perhaps later,' she had replied.

'Are you afraid?' I had continued.

'Afraid?' she scornfully repeated – proudly raising her head – 'I'm an American citizen – they cannot touch me now! Yes,' she had continued in milder tones, 'I would love to meet my family – I am so lonely at times, but I would not care to live in Archangel or Leningrad. I hardly remember them. I was barely three years old when my mother took off with me to Siberia.

'The place,' she continued, 'I would really love to see is Ukraine. There I could live and die! I remember how beautiful was the Dnieper, and there is no city in the world lovelier than Kiev. I spent the best part of my childhood in Ukraine and if it had not been for the war would still be there. I often think about it and long to see it but in my heart I know that this will never happen.'

On the last evening of Olga's stay with us we both wrote a letter to Evgenie. The letters were posted on the following day. On that morning, with Geroge driving and accompanied by Ronald, we set off for Prestwick. Arriving rather early, the time was spent having coffee and strolling around. The 'plane was leaving on time. After the call and fond farewells we watched the long line of passengers walking up to the aircraft and in their midst the small figure of my cousin, soon to vanish out of sight. We have never met again but, as I write these lines in this year of 1995, our correspondence still continues.

June 1985

Dear Jenya,

This morning I was very happy to receive the postcard which you and Olga sent to me from Chew Magna. It is so good to know that you and Olga have met up together.

The view of Chew Magna is very interesting to us. It shows a very lovely village and Michael and his family must enjoy living there. I now await the two letters you have promised to send with all the details of Olga's stay and just wish that I could have been with you. To travel abroad has been a longing that has stayed with me over many years, a longing which I now know can never be realised as after all there is very little time left. I am not so young and feel my years these days.

Your country, Jenya, has everything. What I cannot understand is why we, who work like bees, have so little. You tell me that you have many people who are unemployed but receive what is called 'unemployment benefit'. We have no such allowances and no unemployed apart from drunks and hooligans who do not want to work. For the average man or woman to be unemployed would be a disaster unless it was a health problem in which case there is an allowance.

Just now all our family are in the country. Sergei, during his vacation, is working hard on his cottage. It is difficult to get all the materials he requires so progress is slow and will probably take some years before that cottage is finished.

Natasha with Evgenie and little Alick are staying in her father-in-law's cottage which we understand is spacious and there are masses of all kinds of fruit and vegetables all grown and tended by the old man who lives there alone. Elena and I have no cottage to go to and will content ourselves with walks in our local countryside, accompanied by our animals!

My brother Shurick came last week from Moscow and stayed with us two nights prior to going on to Vicka's cottage, where he will carry out some repairs. Vicka is not so able now and her husband is not keeping well.

I have to say my brother Shurick is a very kind-hearted man – always very cheerful and willing to help. Yet he is the one who has had the hardest life of us all, having been handed over like a puppy to a friend by our mother when she set off to Siberia with three-year-old Olga to join my banished step-father. We always enjoy Shurick's company and were sorry when he left.

After his departure, as I was feeling a bit unsettled I decided to visit the docks. It is a place I go to now and again as all the bustle there, the departures and arrivals of ships reminds me of my own sailing days which I so unhappily gave up for something alien to my heart.

They know me well in these docks. The workers, the sailors and the skippers like to pass a few words with me. There was a ship setting off that day and as I stood admiring the modern lines of this beauty, so different from my old *Gostorg*, so tragically lost in the stormy waters of the Arctic, two young sailors ran past. 'Come with us, Grandad,' they called hurrying up the gangway, 'we are off to the tropics!' 'Wait till I pack my bag!' I replied and stamped my feet pretending I was running.

They laughed, waved their hands and vanished out of sight. I hung around for a while in the hope of seeing this handsome ship slowly, majestically, commence her journey to those distant longed-for lands – but, having promised Elena to return in time for our evening meal, regretfully left the scene.

I am writing this in the living-room, with the door open into our balcony where Elena is engaged in her favourite ploy of transplanting seedlings, watering the flowers and fussing around our lemon tree which was grown from a seed planted twenty-two years ago!

The days are warm and sunny. We are enjoying our walks through the adjoining countryside where the trees are green and everything seems young and fresh. The White Nights are back again. They remind me of Archangel, but there they were lovelier than here. I still remember the haunting silence, broken by the voices on the river, the sun gliding on the opposite shore. How beautiful it all was.

I was hoping to go there this summer, but Elena will not allow me. If my health permits I shall go next year. I would enjoy so much to have a stroll in the birch avenue beside the beloved Dvina, pay my respects to our departed relatives and perchance meet some old friend.

This has been a rather long letter. It is time to stop. I am looking forward so much to these two letters and will be running down to that box in the hope of finding them there. The deliveries vary so much and I might be lucky.

Pass on my best wishes to Ronald and all the members of the family. Elena sends her love.

I embrace and kiss you.

Evgenie

Author's Note

I was not aware when I received the above letter that it was the last one Evgenie wrote to me, and was therefore, as usual, happy to receive the envelope with the familiar writing – never dreaming that both Evgenie and Elena had identical handwriting and that the letter written by Elena contained the tragic news of my cousin's death.

July 1985

Dear Jenya, (Elena wrote)

The two letters from you and Olga arrived on 6 July but did not find my beloved husband alive, as he had died two days earlier, that is on 4 July at 3.20 in the afternoon.

We had our lunch as usual, after which, saying that he had a headache, he decided to lie down. I was in the kitchen washing the dishes when I heard his laboured breathing and ran to find him rolling in agony on the sofa and complaining about a severe pain in his head. I immediately rushed to the telephone and phoned for the doctor but, on returning to him, found he was already unconscious. I lifted his head and held him in my arms, but after a sudden deep breath my beloved husband died. Three minutes later the doctor arrived and told me there was nothing he could do. For me, Jenya, this is a terrible loss. I would have wished that I had been the first to go, but to everyone there is their own time to die and nothing can be done about it. He was buried in the same cemetery as his mother.

For us all, this death was quite unexpected as only a few weeks earlier, when he attended the clinic for his routine therapy and medicine, the doctor, after a thorough examination, told him that his health was good and there was no need for further treatment. I remember when he came back he was so happy – threw his hat down and said 'We live again!' – and now this sudden death.

We held the family service in the church and forty days later had the second service according to the Orthodox Church in which I was brought up. I am now alone, Jenya. Our children lead their own lives. I have my sister, but no one can replace my beloved husband. It is difficult to face up to this grief – this loneliness.

How he always longed for your letters and how happy he was to receive them and how anxious he became if there was an unusual delay.

Please, dear Jenya, write to me.

I kiss you,

Elena

Author's Note

I did write back and our correspondence continues, but not at the same level as with my late cousin.

In conclusion, I should like to say that, having read Evgenie's letters over and over, I decided to translate them and in this way portray the way of life endured by my relatives under Soviet rule, from which I with my Scots mother and brother, miraculously escaped in the year 1920.

Chapter 5

RETURN TO ARCHANGEL

FIVE YEARS ON, my book, *The House by the Dvina* is still going strong. Letters continue to arrive from all the corners of the world, as far away as Australia, Canada, America and South Africa. Many are from Russians who, after fleeing from the scourge of communism, found safety in foreign lands where they settled down to a way of life so different from what they had known in Russia.

As there are hardly any Russians left of my generation, the letters are from their descendants, some of whom refer to me as their 'Aunt Jenya' which I find rather pleasing.

My only connection with Russia is the correspondence between Elena and her family in Leningrad and although my son George keeps prophesying that the book will one day reach Archangel, to me such an event would be nothing short of a miracle! Yet I have discovered throughout my long life that fate at times will spring a surprise. So it happened when one morning in late November 1989 I received a letter with the magic postmark of 'Arhangelsk' on the envelope. The writer was a Tanya Nikolayevna Klushina — head of the Foreign Literature Department of the Dobrolubova Library in Arhangel. I could hardly believe the words which in my excitement seemed to leap up to me:

Dear Mrs Fraser,

This past summer I had the chance to meet a Mrs Anne Bragg from Portland (M.E.) who had spent her early childhood in Archangel and was now revisiting our town with a group of friends. During her visit she presented our library with your book *The House by the Dvina*. I fell in love with the little girl on the cover, took the book home and read it the whole night through, never sleeping, until I finished it in the morning. Your book has moved me deeply and brought back my own childhood which was spent in the Forties in a little settlement south of Archangel. My life there differed much from yours, but strange as it is, we have much in common in our memories of the past.

I understand from your book you have no relatives in Archangel now, which is a pity, but it could be helped if you should visit us and perhaps meet some acquaintances here.

My sister's family and I want to invite you and some companion to visit Archangel. My sister has a flat with two bedrooms which would be at your disposal. We would like to have you as our guests for a month in the summer. My sister's husband has a car and it would not be difficult to visit all the places dear to your heart. Dear Mrs Fraser, I do hope you will consider all this. I understand you may feel a bit uncomfortable to stay with strangers but you should always bear in mind the fact that we are Russians and I don't think there is a need to describe our warm hearts and our hospitality.

Here are some facts abour our family. My name is Tanya Klushina and I am forty-two years old. I live with my son aged sixteen. His name is Kyrill. He studies to become a motor mechanic.

My sister Svetlana is five years younger than me. She has a family of her own. Her husband, Mikhail Korobeinikov is a mechanic on a river boat. They have two sons – Dima ten years old and Arteim twelve. They live in Solombala. In case there is some need of an official invitation, please write to me and I shall do my best.

Dear Mrs Fraser, with all my heart I should like to do something that could please you! Please come to us and be our guest. Remember if Mrs Bragg was not afraid of her long journey across these oceans to visit her birthland – why not you! I wish you health and happiness and await your reply.

Tanya

I was so overwhelmed by this letter written in such perfect English that I read it over and over again as did my husband Ronald and our family.

The last letter I received from Archangel had been written by my Uncle Yura almost six decades earlier! He wrote saying that if we should meet again he would open a bottle of champagne.

This might have taken place if it hadn't been for the killer monster in the Kremlin who, sixteen years after Lenin's seizure of power, decided to execute the remaining White Guard officers, by then engaged in peaceful occupations. Yura, aware of the approaching doom, shot himself. This purge took place during the terrible Thirties, but now we had Mr Gorbachev and his *Glasnost* – allowing people to speak and write as they wished. Yet wonderful as Tanya's invitation was, we pondered whether we should accept it or not. Certain doubts still lingered from the past. Also, experienced travellers as we both were, we found the three flights necessary to reach Archangel rather daunting for our advanced years. In the midst of these long discussions, a second letter arrived, even more startling than the first:

The Town Council of Archangel

The Society of International Friendship – 'We and the World' – invite Mr and Mrs Ronald Fraser to visit Archangel for the duration of four weeks on any chosen summer month (June, July, August) in this year of 1990. The Society guarantees to cover all expenses during your stay in Russia.

The President of the Regional Committee.................. H.A. Juravlev
Secretary.. C. Andreyef
The President of the Society – 'We and the World'.... O. Pavlov

With all doubts dispelled I immediately wrote to the Town Council of Archangel expressing my thanks for their kind invitation and informing them that our visit would take place in the month of July.

We then proceeded to request the Soviet Embassy in London to grant us the necessary visas, never realising that we were entering an enervating struggle with bureaucracy! At last the many forms received were completed and returned to the Embassy with the specified fees. We settled down to wait – and wait – and wait. No acknowledgement was received and sadly the Embassy would not even answer incoming 'phone calls!

Meanwhile our son Michael decided to accompany us to Leningrad to meet our relatives and have a look at Peter's City. He applied to Intourist in Glasgow for his ticket and visa and in a matter of two weeks received both. Next, he also, through Tanya Klushina, to his great surprise and delight, received an invitation from the Archangel government to join us, something which surprised and delighted him.

In June, Ian Taylor of the United Television Artists, who had been engaged by the BBC to produce a documentary of our trip to Archangel, arrived at the house with his crew to film an interview with me. He also filmed a talk I was invited to give when opening an exhibition in the Albert Institute in Dundee. I was not to see him again until I stepped off the 'plane in Archangel. We were now into June and there was still no sign of the visas. Remembering my unfortunate visit to Russia in 1972 I was beginning to think that the Soviet Embassy was not overjoyed at the prospect of my visiting Archangel. The situation was especially desperate as already arrangements were made to stay with my cousin's widow, Elena, who was determined that we should spend some days with her prior to our departure for Archangel.

As a last resort Ronald decided to enlist the services of Intourist in Glasgow and on 30 June they phoned to tell us the glad news that the visas had arrived.

A week later we embarked on the first part of our journey. As there were no flights from Edinburgh to Leningrad, or any other capitals in Eastern Europe, we flew to London, where we put up in a hotel and on the following morning boarded a 'plane to Leningrad. After an uneventful flight followed by a very prolonged taxiing on arrival we eventually disembarked at the terminal.

Prior to leaving, aware of the great scarcity of various commodities, we had indulged in an orgy of buying presents not only for our relatives but also for friends known and unknown in Archangel. Now, as we approached the customs, we were not relishing the prospect of having our cases examined.

Michael, however, solved the problem. Our nine cases were loaded on to a long trolley by an elderly porter to whom Michael gave a dollar bill and by some means or other, in spite of his limited knowledge of Russian, conveyed to him that he would give him another dollar bill when we were through the customs.

'No sooner said than done!' Our porter pushed the trolley past the customs dismissing voluble protests by the officials with a wave of his hand and helped our waiting friends to load up the waiting cars.

Standing waiting outside were two lovely young women holding beautiful bouquets. They were Natasha, with her husband Evgenie and 'young Elena' (as she was known) and Sergei. In this way, after many years of exchanging letters with my late cousin Evgenie, I was now getting to know his children. After a joyful meeting we set off for the flat where my cousin's widow, also called Elena, was awaiting our arrival. Ronald and I travelled with Natasha and Evgenie, who was driving a battered Lada, while Michael went with Elena and Sergei in an equally battered taxi. Elena (senior) lived a long way from the airport. She had long since given up her spacious house to Natasha and was now living in a modest flat of two rooms situated in a pleasant district close to a large lake and open countryside.

We enjoyed the long run and it was one way of getting closer and better acquainted. During our conversation, Evgenie, perhaps conscious of the battered Lada, explained that he had borrowed it from a friend as his own completely new car bought four months earlier had been stolen the previous week. To Ron's enquiry if he had got anything from his insurance cover, Evgenie explained that he had bought it in the black market the way so many cars were bought and had no papers. He was now on the look out for another car!

On arrival we were met by Elena and her two grandchildren. Before me was a woman of medium height, round faced with blue eyes, who warmly embraced and kissed me. The two little boys kept jumping around in great excitement. The elder of the two, Rodion or 'Rodie', almost seven years old, was a good-looking, sturdy child. He also showed he was highly intelligent as, after persuasion by his grandmother, he gave us a recitation of *Frère Jaques* in three languages – English, French and Russian. Aleksandr or 'Alick', seven months younger than his cousin, was of a quieter disposition, but also very talented as we learned when we visited Natasha.

Another welcoming member of the family was Aisha, a miniature poodle puppy, who greatly amused the boys by prancing on her hind legs and pulling Ron's handkerchief out of his pocket! Aliska, her predecessor and winner of gold medals in dog shows, died when having pups. The pups did not survive. Their cat Yashka, who used to accompany Elena and Evgenie on their walks, had also passed away and Elena, finding life very empty, had acquired Aisha and become passionately attached to her.

On the arrival of Sergei, Elena and Michael the family was complete and it was time to present our gifts. We had brought several articles not available in Leningrad, to the great delight of the children. Their elders were likewise happy, but perhaps a little bit embarrassed, especially Natasha who, although enthralled with her shoes, exclaimed – 'God, I feel like a beggar!' We were likewise presented with beautiful, painted lacquer boxes of the Palek school, a beautiful amber necklace and a small antique ikon.

With the exchange of gifts completed, there followed the usual Russian custom of gathering round the table. Elena had been working hard preparing a selection of dishes and salads. Natasha carried in a boiling samovar and so commenced a session that lasted well into the night. The younger members of the family, knowing very little concerning the past, asked many questions and were surprised to learn about the various events that took place in those distant years. We were unexpectedly joined by the arrival of my cousin Aleksandr, better known as 'Shurick', who, wishing to meet me, had travelled from Moscow. I never knew Shurick before as he was born after I left Russia. In spite of his terrible suffering at the hands of the Nazis, as a prisoner of war, Shurick was very warm and cheerful. After the war he landed in Moscow where he married, raised a family and was now working for the government as a builder.

As the party continued beyond midnight, it was discovered that the hotel where Michael was booked was situated at the other end of the town – too far for him to travel at this late hour. He therefore spent the night sharing our bedroom sleeping on a couch bed.

In the forenoon, Sergei and Elena arrived and took Michael and Ronald away to register Michael's arrival in the Karelia Hotel where he should have booked in the previous day. Fortunately his explanations were accepted and after checking into his room, he left with Ronald, Sergei and Elena to visit the Peter and Paul fortress. Meanwhile Elena (senior) and I set off for one of the government offices where it was necessary for Elena to have our stay with her registered. After spending some time in the waiting room we were shown into a room where a friendly young woman was sitting at her desk. Following a few questions and some pleasant conversation we rose to leave but as we were leaving I observed Elena placing some roubles on the desk which the young lady calmly transferred into the drawer beside her. Nothing was said, but I came away wondering if this was a fee or 'baksheesh'.

On our return back to the house, Elena and I spent a quiet hour together talking about the sad loss of my cousin Evgenie or 'Jenya' as she referred to him. She showed me the special album he kept where every picture sent by me was placed in meticulous order, with the date and place where it was taken. 'You will never know how much your letters meant to him,' Elena told me. 'Your descriptions of where you have travelled and lived were of absorbing interest to him. You were also the only link with the past. Through you he discovered that the purpose of your babushka's amazing journey to St Petersburg was to plead with the Tsar to free your grandfather from Siberia. Babushka was too afraid to talk about anything connected with the past which might have got her family into trouble.'

Elena also pointed out the pictures on the wall which her husband painted. I had no idea that Evgenie was such a gifted artist. There were three pictures painted from memory of the experience in Novaya Zemlya – one of the ship *Gostorg*, the second of it foundering in the storm and the third of the terrible trek across Novaya Zemlya, complete with sledges and dogs. We took small copies later but they could never do justice to the originals. Another example of painstaking work was a model of a galleon built in Archangel by Peter the Great. Every minute detail is there and according to Elena, Evgenie laboured for many months to reach the perfection he desired.

Elena and I got to know each other as we sat talking together. She told me that, like many others, she had suffered during the siege of Leningrad, had lost her mother from starvation and that the only relative to survive was her sister with whom she keeps in contact.

In the late afternoon Seroyzha and Elena brought back Ronald and Michael and after some refreshment returned to their flat. Later, following an invitation from Natasha, we set off in a taxi to visit her. Michael sat in front beside the driver while Elena, Ronald and I were in the back. Between Elena and Ronald was Aisha placed inside a little bag which Ron discovered to his cost was not waterproof! After a long journey we eventually arrived in Shotman Street and were warmly welcomed by Natasha and Evgenie. I felt a little sad, remembering that it was from this flat that my cousin Evgenie faithfully corresponded with me for over thirteen years. He had always hoped for Ronald and me to visit them and had actually enquired from the authorities about permission to put us up but so many objections were made nothing came of it. Now here I was, yet never having dreamt that such a thing would happen.

The flat was spacious and well furnished complete with a piano and a thirty-three-inch Panasonic television with video-recorder. Evgenie is a composer and does quite well from his records. After being persuaded by Elena to play he sat down at the piano and gave a brilliant variation of *Moscow Nights* much enjoyed by us all. Then little Alick, with some coaxing, scrambled on to the stool and played a piece of music that might well have been difficult for many an adult. We were quite fascinated watching these little fingers with great skill and confidence gliding over the keys. Later, when invited to the table, we discovered that Natasha was an excellent cook. There was a rich selection of *zakuskis* followed by a lavish meat course, a choice of sweets and a liberal supply of vodka and champagne.

We had looked forward to hearing Evgenie's records but sadly that part of the evening was ruined by Aisha's wild non-stop barking drowning out all sound. Fortunately, there was a short respite which allowed us to enjoy a talk together prior to leaving. With Evgenie succeeding in finding a taxi we left after midnight and after dropping Michael at the Karelia Hotel carried on home and thankfully got to bed about two a.m.

The following morning our ever faithful Sergei and Elena came to take us to the Hermitage where we met up with Evgenie and Michael. It was our last chance to see something of Leningrad as we were leaving the next day for Archangel.

I had visited the Hermitage during my unfortunate visit in 1972, but as our guide had rushed us through from room to room I remembered very little. Now we were able to stroll at our leisure and admire the magnificence of each room and also a wonderful exhibition of articles from the Etruscan age. Later we set off to find a 'Berezka' shop where I hoped to buy some gifts for friends at home and perhaps something for myself. Evgenie, who knew every 'Berezka' in town, took us to the one he thought was the best. There I bought a few presents and also treated myself to a beautiful china teapot depicting cockerels painted in gold and scarlet. I also acquired two mugs and saucers with the same delightful design which are treasured to this day.

Cockerels have a symbolic significance for Russians which, I have heard, is due to a religious connection. They are not only painted or carved on wood but can also be found embroidered on linen, towels, teacloths and around the hems of sarafans, as on the one I wore during my childhood. It was bordered with a row of scarlet cockerels on a turquoise blue background.

Meanwhile, after spending a great deal of time in the 'Berezka' we found it difficult to find a place to have lunch until Evgenie succeeded in persuading a restaurant owner to let us in. The upshot was an excellent meal. When Ronald asked Evgenie what was the secret of his success, he explained that twenty-five years ago he used to play the piano in this restaurant and the owner still remembered him.

It was now late afternoon and as we had promised Elena (senior) to be back in time to meet some friends due to arrive in the early evening, we had to find a taxi immediately. This proved to be very difficult, but Evgenie, ever resourceful, managed to stop one. After saying our goodbyes we thankfully got in and duly arrived at the house.

It so happened that this was the evening of what is known as the 'White Night' celebrations when all the youth of Leningrad gathered on the banks of the Neva to sing songs, to meet up with each other and generally enjoy themselves. After Seroyzha and Elena suggested that Michael might like to join in, the three of them went off together.

The friends who duly arrived turned out to be Nina and her daughter Masha. Nina, the daughter of my late step-uncle Sergei who, with his wife and son starved to death during the siege of Leningrad, was the sole surviver of the family, fortunate to be picked up by a group of charitable people dedicated to saving and bringing up orphaned children. In spite of her tragic experience and recently losing her husband, she was a cheerful friendly woman as was her daughter Masha – a tall handsome girl. The three of us joyfully embraced and kissed each other with Ronald following suit.

I was a little puzzled by Masha's great height and broad shoulders, so completely dwarfing her dainty mother. She kept reminding me of someone somewhere, but I could not remember whom until it suddenly dawned on me that she had inherited the exact build of her great-grandfather – Doctor Alexander Popov, my step-grandfather – who was unusually tall and broadly built. How strange is heredity which can go back for three generations!

We spent a happy time reminiscing about the sad and happy events in the family and were later joined by Shurick who called to see us once again prior to our departure for Archangel. The party broke up earlier than usual as it was necessary for us to sort out our luggage in readiness for the departure to Archangel.

In the morning we were awakened by Aisha jumping up on the bed and licking my face. After breakfast Michael arrived. The White Night festivities had turned out to be a complete failure. The young people had gathered as usual on the banks of the Neva and were all set to enjoy themselves when suddenly the skies darkened, followed by a heavy downpour. Everyone rushed for shelter. Seroyzha was lucky to find a café on one of the side streets where they spent some time before finding a taxi and dropping Michael at his hotel.

Soon after Michael, Natasha arrived with Evgenie and little Alick to bid us *adieu* prior to setting off for the countryside where Evgenie's father had a cottage. Their visit was followed by the anxiously awaited arrival of Tanya Klushina who was to accompany us on our flight to Archangel. After many months of correspondence I had at times wondered what sort of person this

Tanya would be and was delighted to discover that here was a good-looking woman with a friendly manner, perhaps in her early forties. We immediately felt perfectly at ease as if we had known each other for a long time. Soon the taxi arrived. We said goodbye to our relatives, promising to see them again on our way back to Scotland and set off for the airport. There to our surprise we were met by Seroyzha and Elena with a bouquet of flowers. How wonderfully kind I thought were all my relatives.

Soon we were airborne on our way to Archangel – my Archangel.

*   *   *   *

Travelling by plane in Russia I have discovered can be a nerve-racking experience. Facing me across the table, which was covered with numerous packages, was a pleasant-looking young woman. Under the table was a large, heavy basket which was pressing on my toes and causing great discomfort, and did not encourage any exchange of pleasantries. Ronald likewise was confronted by a youth who had stretched his long legs right under Ron's seat. Retaliation was simple and sure. Ron simply placed his feet on the offending legs and the owner with an expression of pained surprise swiftly drew them back. Not a word was spoken!

Across the passage, Michael and Tanya sitting together were enjoying their conversation.

In distant times, the journey by train used to take two days and two nights. Now by 'plane we reached Archangel in a matter of an hour! I was directed to leave first. Facing me as I came down the steps were four women dressed in sarafans, offering the traditional loaf of black bread and salt to the accompaniment of a welcoming song. This was totally unexpected. Deeply touched and at a loss for words, I tried to express my thanks and to tell them how good it was to be back after an absence of seventy years. I was surrounded by people – some offering bouquets, some introducing themselves, some asking questions. A car, lent by the local Council, drew up and complete with flowers and the loaf of black bread, we all gratefully scrambled in. Thus began our stay in Archangel!

I had no idea where the airport was situated and did not recognise anything until we reached the bridge to Solombala when everything that I had known before came back again.

The bridge to Solombala Island stretches from a place called Kuznechiha ['the place of the blacksmiths'] which lies to the north of the city. It was in Solombala that Peter the Great built his first ship and sailed it across the White Sea. As I hardly ever visited Solombala during my childhood I did not expect to recognise anything there. After crossing the bridge we halted in front of a high-rise building. Tanya's sister Svetlana lived on the third floor, but she and her husband Misha and their two boys were away visiting their mother in the country.

The flat was spacious and well furnished, consisting of two bedrooms with twin beds and fitted wardrobes. The living-room was likewise spacious as was the hall. The well-laid-out kitchen was large enough to hold a table where each morning we had our breakfast. In the bathroom there was a bath, shower and washing machine and adjoining, a separate toilet. Everything portrayed the abode of a house-proud housewife.

On arriving we found the living-room was crowded with people who came to welcome us and amongst them I discovered my only relative – Cousin Alexei – the son of my late step-uncle Yura who had died so tragically during the terrible Thirties. It was Alexei Popov, I learned later, who, being in charge of the airport, had arranged the reception and many of the events which followed. Meanwhile we all sat down to a lavish spread accompanied by wine, vodka and numerous toasts. It was a very free and happy gathering which it has to be said was only made possible by Michael Gorbachev's *glasnost.*

As the party drew to a close and everyone gradually dispersed, Michael was invited by Oleg Pavlov to join him and some other friends to spend the night aboard a motor launch on the Dvina, something that many young people enjoyed during the White Nights.

Meanwhile we gladly retreated to our bedroom where we might have had a more peaceful night if it had not been for the mosquitoes which flew in from the adjoining balcony, something I did not think was possible situated as we were on the third floor.

In the morning Michael returned in time for breakfast having spent a wonderful night with the boys sailing up and down the river. During the forenoon a van arrived and took us across the bridge to the mainland and up to the part where facing the river once stood our house. Another building was now standing in the grounds but there was no trace of the house in which I had spent my early childhood. Hoping perhaps to be allowed to have a walk around the place, Michael and I tried to enter, but the gates were securely locked and all we could see was a grassy expanse and some stunted trees and bushes in front of a building which Tanya informed us was a hospital.

Determined to get close to my beloved Dvina, I went down some steps – new to me – and stood at the edge of the river. Great changes had taken place. In my time, from the road above, the bank had sloped down to the water's edge. There, between the stones, various plants would grow – many of them edible. I stood remembering that hungry summer of 1920 when our 'Companiya', as we named ourselves, spent happy hours searching for something to eat – the tiny wild peas, sorrel leaves, angelica and much prized small wild strawberries.

Now, in place of the bank there stood a vertical concrete wall fronted by a wide sandy beach stretching down to the river. Untold tons of sand must have been dumped to create this beautiful *plage*. Although at one time much enjoyed by the town's folk and visitors, the river had now become polluted and people were not encouraged to go swimming.

As often happens in Mother Russia all such warnings were ignored and close to where I stood an elderly gentleman was enjoying his morning swim. Encouraged by his example I removed my shoes and stockings and waded up to my knees in the no longer crystal clear waters. Directly opposite lay the island of Kegostrov bringing back memories of how, in the early spring, my playmates and I would ski across the frozen river to bring back catkins from the willow thickets in time for Palm Sunday, better known in the North as 'Willow Sunday'.

The most beautiful feature of Archangel, known in my time as 'The Boulevard', where we continued our walk, consists of three long rows of high birch trees running parallel to the river. From the sea wall to the first line of trees is a wide concrete pavement where the children can play or cycle free from danger as there is no access for motor traffic. Next to this are the two further birch-lined avenues and then the busy main road. The birches are lovely at all times whether in the summer or in the winter dressed in sparkling frost. I have to add that the northern birches are more beautiful than their sister trees grown in warmer climes. Tall and slender with curly heads and silver-white trunks, they are often compared to maidens from some ancient Russian fairy tale.

It was here while strolling along the avenue that a young woman who approached me turned out to be a reporter, asked many questions and was interested to learn about my childhood in Archangel. She was joined by another lady, who was not a reporter but was eager to meet me and had asked Ron's permission to do so, which was something I found quite amusing. We had a long talk together but as it was now time for us to have some lunch we left the river front for the centre of the town where Tanya guided us to the 'Polyarni Restaurant'. There we enjoyed a very good lunch for which, including Ian and his team who had been filming all my movements, we paid the modest price of thirty-seven roubles! We then went back to Solombala, only to return shortly after to the cemetery where a memorial service in honour of my father and all my relatives was due to take place.

At the cemetery we were met by Father Nikolai a gentle, kindly man. He was accompanied by the deacon and two ladies – members of the choir.

On the ground belonging to the family, the tombstones in red granite dating back to the eighteenth century were still standing. The one erected to my grandfather who had died in 1890 was lying in two pieces, either vandalised or cracked by frost. To the right were the simple crosses erected to my relations who had died after our departure for Scotland.

The service and the accompanying singing were deeply moving. I stood beside my father's grave, remembering how he had longed for us and begged for our return which of course had been impossible, and now I was back after seventy long years. Standing in the background was a small group consisting of Ronald, Michael and Tanya and beside them Alexei, with his son Alesha.

Some memorial services are sad, difficult to bear and in this instance too painful to describe.

After the service we visited the little church standing beside the cemetery. Having recently been done up it was beautiful inside with several rare ikons presented by the parishioners. After a pleasant conversation with Father Nikolai we left the church and went to Alexei's house to meet the other members of his family. Michael, to his regret, was unable to accept the invitation as he had already arranged with Oleg Pavlov for some long trip up the river.

Alexei lived in a spacious and well-furnished flat. There we met his wife Shura, a good-looking and pleasant woman. It was difficult to imagine that this same lady had been a partisan, fighting the Germans, hiding in the woods under constant threat of death and, at the end of the war, being decorated for bravery.

Shura had prepared an excellent meal complete with champagne and vodka. Gathered round the table were his son Alesha, with his wife and daughter, Alexei's daughter Irina and six-year-old granddaughter Marina, a very lively child and talented pianist who was obviously her grandfather's pride and delight!

While we were talking together it suddenly occurred to me – what would my young Uncle Yura have thought had he been able to look into the future and seen me sitting together with his son and family. Strange are the ways of God, as they say in Russia.

At the end of a happy evening Alexei escorted us to the bus stop where we boarded the bus and were soon safely back home in Solombala.

During the following fortnight we continued crossing and recrossing the bridge. Every evening we were being lavishly entertained by our newly acquired friends. Long discussions, singing and even dancing went on well into the night.

One morning we were invited to meet the members of the local government. We duly arrived at their office and were welcomed by three young men who invited me to join them at the table with Ron, Michael and Tanya sitting nearby watching the proceedings. As not one of my hosts could speak in English the conversation took place in Russian. Never having been in Scotland and knowing very little about it, they asked many questions and displayed a great interest in everything I told them. Politics were barely mentioned and when they were I made no secret of the fact that I was not a communist. As

Mihail Gorbachev did not approve of alcohol being offered during interviews, we were served with chocolate and *morse* (a refreshing drink prepared from cranberries). My interrogators were pleasant young men so it was all very congenial. At the end of the meeting, each of us was presented with books and tokens of Archangelsk and we parted with mutual expressions of goodwill.

During my stay I found all the people I met were always friendly and hospitable. Often when strolling on the streets I was approached by strangers wishing to talk to me and offering presents of such things as little figures of samoyeds, painted bowls, embroidered aprons and so on. To me, they were the same warm-hearted people as I had known in my childhood.

What I did not expect to find was the complete transformation of Archangel. At one time the town held a certain charm. On the main street, known as Troitski Prospect, as well as on the river front and other streets, stood the beautiful wooden houses belonging to various citizens, but one by one they, along with the cathedral and churches, were removed and replaced by multi-storeyed buildings standing in line one after another and all of the same bleak design, the sight of which does not caress the eyes. At the same time, it has to be admitted that the boon of having constant hot and cold running water plus central heating has made life more comfortable for the greater part of the population. Strange as it may seem I am compelled to add that there are still some ladies who do not believe that clothes are properly rinsed until they can be taken to the river.

What breaks the harshness of these modern streets is the pleasing sight of the tall birches, standing knee-deep in grass and bordering the footpaths. Their purpose, I was told, was to absorb the poisonous fumes from the traffic – a concept which was new to me!

Our friend Yuri Barashkov, an architect whom we met in Archangel, in his book *Nostalgia for the Wooden Town* expresses regret over the loss of these lovely old houses but also admits it was inevitable as the population had increased from forty thousand at the start of the First World War to the present day figure of almost half a million. The reason for this great increase was because so many people moved from the south to better positions with higher salaries in the Arctic regions or had been banished to Archangel during the communist regime following a term of hard labour in Siberia. Such a fate was experienced by my cousin Olga's step-father who, after serving a term in Siberia, was sent to Archangel and later returned to his village in Ukraine where during the terrible Thirties he was executed.

The days continued to be warm and sunny. On one occasion, we decided to explore the town and perhaps buy some gifts for our friends at home. However, on arriving in the centre of the town we did not notice any shops beyond one multiple store. Inside, apart from some excellent cameras, there was nothing worth buying – some tawdry clothing, poor quality fur hats and a selection of useless objects. More rewarding was the craft shop selling locally produced articles – beautifully painted bowls, carvings in wood, hand knitted shawls, scarves, fur-lined gloves and attractive miniature figures of Eskimos and animals such as abound in the Arctic regions. After buying a few items we continued on our way.

What we found puzzling throughout our stay was that, although we were fed very well and in fact too much at times, nowhere did we see a single shop which sold provisions. Here and there we came across stalls selling vegetables or fruit and on one corner I saw a kiosk selling vodka with some men standing around. 'Where do you buy all your food?' I asked Tanya. 'We do not buy – we get,' was Tanya's calm reply.

I was remembering my cousin's daughter Natasha in Leningrad telling me that there were no shops in Archangel and that, when she and her group in 1972 were sent there to give a performance, they had to take all their food with them. I repeated this sad tale to Tanya and to my surprise she agreed that this was indeed so. 'Why should we feed all these outsiders?' she commented. 'We have enough to do feeding our own people.' We did, however, hear later that there was a small market place somewhere in the background. There is a current joke that the Russians had invented a new system by which goods passed straight from the producer to the fridge without going near any shops. Yes – much had changed. Only the Dvina flowing serenely between her green banks remained as beautiful as ever.

What were excellent and worth a visit were the museums. Especially wonderful was the display of exquisite carvings in ivory – such as on the cover of an ancient bible, beautiful tiny figures of chessmen, jewel-boxes, bracelets, necklaces etc. Excellent also was the display of fine lace in another museum. Here we admired lovely tablecloths, dresses, coats, bed-covers all as fine as cobwebs woven in a special way by the talented women of the north.

The pride of place, however, for the people of Archangel is the miniature creation of the town itself by her gifted son, Zasima Petrovich Kalashnikov. He had laboured over his brainchild for five long years so that the people of Archangel could see how once their town looked prior to its shameful destruction under the communist regime. This amazing reproduction, stretching for thirty-seven metres, occupies a large hall in the Marine Institute. It is visited not only by the locals but by masses of people from other parts of Russia.

Everything can be seen here – every house, every building, the schools, the cathedral, so wantonly destroyed, all the churches, gardens and trees and even the line of the river. I myself was deeply touched to recognise our old home and to know that it hasn't vanished for ever. And, as if all that was not enough, on the walls can be seen a collection of beautiful paintings created by Zasima depicting various scenes of the north.

Sadly, however, this genius who had given so much to his town was now dying from some strange affliction. His wife, following Zasima's request, invited Ronald and me to visit him. We called the following afternoon. Zasima and his wife lived in one of the better flats in a building with an imposing entrance. Inside we were met by Mrs Kalashnikova, who introduced us to her daughter and two lovely young granddaughters who had arrived on a visit from Murmansk. After some small talk the daughter showed us into her father's bedroom. Zasima was lying, unable to walk or speak, but still in possession of his sight and hearing. This daughter, who was the only one who could understand what her father was saying, informed me 'He knows all about your book, but would like you to tell him again the story of the little pig!' Although taken aback, I sat down beside him and began to relate how on one summer morning in the year 1918 while my brother and I were searching for mushrooms in the garden we found to our amazement a small pig rooting in the bushes. We had carried it between us to the house where we suggested to my father we should keep it and perhaps start breeding from it and in this way never go hungry. My father, however, along with my Uncle Sanya had other ideas. The little pig was trustingly left in their hands, only to appear two days later on the table in the shape of tender chops, succulent quarters, and various tasty bits. We had a feast such as we hadn't enjoyed for a considerable time. The following day a young man appeared at our back door. He came from the adjoining property where an important commissar had arrived from the country along with his pig. He was more than grieved when he discovered that the pig had vanished. It was last seen burrowing beside our mutual wall. After a superficial search in the garden he called again to inform us that on the following morning, with the help of some soldiers, a thorough search of the garden would take place and if any traces were found there would be trouble! We became terrified, already visualising imprisonment and banishment to Siberia. Providence, however, as the saying goes, works at times in mysterious ways. The following day the ships of the Allied Intervention arrived on the scene and the commissar, with his men, fled up the river.

At the end of this story, Zasima's daughter passed on her father's thanks and his wish that I should go back to the Marine Institute and pick any picture that I fancied. I did so and as I write these lines the lovely painting of an ancient Post House is hanging on our wall, but sadly Zasima is no more.

After my session with him and his daughter, we joined the other members of the family in their living-room where Mrs Kalashnikova had prepared a samovar accompanied by a great variety of sandwiches and cakes. In spite of the overhanging tragedy it was a cheerful gathering. The young granddaughters appeared to enjoy life in Murmansk as there were now schools, clubs, cinemas and discos – a different picture from the barren waste that I remembered from our sojourn there seventy years earlier when we were anxiously searching for a boat that would take us across to Norway. Miraculously, a small trawler appeared on the scene, but for which these lines would never have been written. Eventually, after sailing over stormy seas, we landed safely at Varda.

One evening later we received an invitation from Yuri Barashkov to join him with his wife Tanya for supper. We duly set off for his flat accompanied by Michael and our Tanya. On arriving we were warmly welcomed by Yuri and introduced to a friend who had come along to meet us. Yuri, passionately fond of music, possesses a great collection of records. We spent the evening listening to these records and talking on various subjects.

Yuri, like many more of his age, was interested to learn about the various aspects of life which took place before and during the Revolution. There are very few people, if any, left in Archangel who had witnessed those stirring events, as so many of the older citizens perished during the last war. I, on the other hand, knew nothing at all about life in Archangel during the years of the Second World War and was surprised to learn that there was very little thought given to the welfare of the citizens and that the starvation there was almost as bad as in Leningrad. Yuri described what a treat it was for him and other children to receive, once a week, a sandwich spread with seal blubber. Such were the many hardships endured – so different from my own war years in India.

We left after midnight travelling back in the Volga limousine provided by Yuri. It was still clear daylight and, as the saying goes, a time when sunrise and sunset meet. The crimson disk of the sun moving slowly behind the island of Kegostrov was casting a rosy glow over the river. There was great activity at the Yachting Club. All the yachts and motor boats of every description were setting off for a night on the river, making the most of the few weeks left of the summer.

'We are not a land of long summers,' Yuri told me, 'not for us are the golden fruits and cherry trees growing outside our cottages. We leave that to the Ukrainians and their God-given climate. We are a land of deep snows, of long dark winter nights, hard frosts and frozen rivers. She belongs to us – we love her.'

During our stay in Archangel there was never a day passed without our being entertained by our loving new friends – yet I sometimes wished I could see again some of the places I knew during my childhood. There were, for instance, the Summer Gardens, with long avenues of trees, a pond where children liked to fish for tadpoles, a restaurant which remained open well into the night and a band that played each afternoon and evening. Best of all was a theatre presenting plays and operas by talented actors and singers who came each summer from St Petersburg and Moscow. It was there that I first listened to *Eugene Onegin, The Queen of Spades* and many other performances. I asked Tanya if the Summer Gardens were still in existence and she said that they were, but one day when I was passing the place where the gates once stood, I saw an ugly building there instead and did not press the matter again. It was possible the garden was behind the building, but it could never have been the same as I remembered it.

Occasionally, when Tanya was required in the library, we would set off for a stroll on our own, usually by the river where there was always something going on to draw our attention. It was on such a morning we came upon a small garden known as The Square where stands a monument on which are inscribed the words 'to the Victims of the Foreign Intervention'.

These words reminded me of an incident which took place in 1919 when a group of soldiers mutinied in the barracks and their leaders were executed by the order of General Ironside – at that time the head of the Allied Intervention forces. This, I may add, created a certain resentment among many Russians including those who were not communists but who did not think it was right that a foreign general should have had the power to execute a Russian soldier.

Further along I saw a tank which, to my amazement, I discovered was the same tank I saw standing helplessly on the main street when on my way to school shortly after the defeat of the White Army in that fatal month in February in 1920. The tanks, along with a group of Russian officers and men trained in the use of the tank, were brought from Britain by the same ice-breaker – the *Canada* – on which I was also travelling along with my mother and brother after a short stay in Scotland. It had been hoped that the tanks would be a decisive factor in the battle against the Bolsheviks, but due to the fuel freezing and the unsuitable ground in the forests they proved to be useless. This tragic error led to the execution of all these fine men and to the town finally falling into the hands of the enemy. In 1920 the victorious Bolsheviks took a horrible revenge by forcing some of the imprisoned officers (including my Uncle Yura) to exhume the bodies of the mutineers, buried in the outskirts of the town, and rebury them in the garden where the monument now stands.

* * * *

Meanwhile time was passing – we were into the middle of July and the end of Michael's leave. On the morning of his last day in Archangel, Tanya's sister Svetlana with her husband Misha arrived from the country. Svetlana, fair-haired and attractive, is the head of a depot for receiving food and other items. There she arranges, sets prices for, and distributes the various articles to other centres in the region. Misha, a friendly man, is an engineer who works on a ship rounding up logs which have broken loose from the timber rafts. Their two young sons were staying with their grandmother in the country and so we never got to know them.

During the forenoon Misha took Michael with Ron and me into town, where Michael wished to buy some gifts for the family in Edinburgh and to say goodbye to his friends. On our return in the afternoon we found that the girls had been busy preparing the food for Michael's farewell party. On the table was a rich selection of *zakuskis* – salads, chicken, meat, fresh strawberries and even *maroshka* – the golden berry that grows in marshes and is almost extinct nowadays. Tanya, on hearing me telling her how we, when young, used to gather the maroshka, had gone to the trouble of finding some.

The 'get together' commenced in the early evening. The first to arrive was Valya Golisheva who spoke perfect English being holder of the Chair of English at Archangel University. The others were Olga Balaganova, Katya Menshikova who, like Tanya Klushina could speak freely in English and also present was Tanya Urchenko who, although a grandmother, liked nothing better than to dance and sing in a lively Russian style. All these girls had entertained us during our stay and had now gathered to bid Michael farewell. Ian Taylor, leaving his camera crew behind, likewise joined the party.

There was a lot of talking, laughter and singing. Valya excelled herself with her knowledge of every song, Russian or English. Michael and Ian presented a duet of popular English songs with Ronald at times joining in.

Some time after midnight the party was over. In the hall were lingering goodbyes, a few jokes and one by one the guests departed. The rest of us went off to bed leaving Michael and Tanya to deal with the dishes. In the early morning Michael popped in to say goodbye to us. Misha, accompanied by Tanya, took him to the airport. Soon he was back in St Petersburg where he was met by Seryozha and Elena. They took him for a last look at the town and later saw him safely off on his flight to London.

It was sad that Michael's leave was all too short as a few days later we had a memorable trip of some forty miles up the river to a place where we enjoyed a picnic.

This was arranged through the auspices of the head of the fish processing factory, Leonid Alexeyevich Sevestianov, who kindly offered to transport us in a spacious fishing vessel. At the appointed hour, along with Ian Taylor and his camera crew, we all assembled on the jetty near the monument to the victims of the intervention to await the arrival of Leonid and his boat.

While we were sitting there, Ronald and I were approached by an elderly gentleman who introduced himself as Captain Novgorodski and told us that during the war he had been connected with the American convoys and at the end of hostilities was presented by them with a medal which he was wanting to present to Ronald – an offer which Ronald politely declined. The captain was a very friendly man who had in his time travelled to such places as Madras and Calcutta. He was anxious we should return to his flat where he wished to present me with a picture of the ice-breaker *Canada* on which I had travelled to Archangel in that disastrous year of 1920. We had to decline his invitation, however, on account of the picnic but promised to see him again prior to our return to Scotland.

Meanwhile, time was passing and there was still no sign of Leonid but as we were beginning to feel a bit anxious, his wife appeared – a rather flamboyant, plump lady dressed in a little white jacket over a red bathing suit which toned in nicely with her curly auburn hair.

It transpired that early in the morning her husband decided to gather mushrooms in a place some distance from Archangel. He had taken his car and promised to return but sadly after gathering his mushrooms and setting off on the return journey the car broke down. However, being within reach of a telephone he told his wife to instruct his assistant to take over and bring us to a certain part where he would join us.

This explanation by 'Madam' was accompanied by expressions of scornful contempt and various Russian proverbs, all directed against the male sex in general and her husband in particular.

Soon we were aboard sailing up the river leaving a foaming wake as we sped on making up for lost time. On our left lay the town, soon to vanish out of sight, on our right the islands, closely knit together. I wondered idly if the villages which I used to visit still existed. There in some *isba* I would sleep in the hayloft above the cattle and spend happy hours in the woods gathering mushrooms and berries.

It was very hot but quite enjoyable between the joking and the laughing and the non-stop flow of humorous comments from our lively hostess.

After some thirty miles or less, we hove-to beside a peaceful sandy beach lying at the bottom of a high sloping cliff, covered in grass and shrubs. From the top, leading down to the water, was a narrow path on which our host, Leonid Alexeiyevitch was coming to join us. I had hoped that the picnic might take place on this lovely beach but apparently there were other plans. Leonid clambered aboard and we continued for a few more miles, eventually running the boat on to a beach on the right bank of the river. The only means of disembarking was to walk down a narrow plank set at an acute angle which I viewed with some dismay, but, with the camera crew reaching up on either side to hold my hand I made it. Ronald and the others gingerly followed – unassisted. Above the river lay a long grassy patch where the girls immediately began to lay out a tablecloth and all the bottles and provisions they had brought with them. The patch was fenced off and beyond it was a grassy field bordered by woods on either side.

Meanwhile I was surprised to see a rowing boat, trailing a net packed with fish, approaching the beach. The net was then emptied into the boat. Here was a great variety of fish – pike, *siga* (of the salmon species) and many others with which the Dvina is so richly endowed. Leonid immediately begun to gut the fish removing heads, tails etc and throwing the refuse into the water to be carried out to sea. A large, two-handled iron drum was cleaned and scrubbed with sand and after putting in the fish along with pepper, salt, bay leaves and dill, and filling it with water from the river, the drum was hung on a branch between two forked sticks above a bonfire.

While all these preparations were going on Ronald decided to have a swim and was joined by 'Madam' who, to our amusement, took his hand and led him down the bank and into the river. As none of the rest of us brought bathing suits we were content to watch the pair swimming which did not last very long as the water was too rough for enjoyment. While Ronald was discreetly changing into his shorts, 'Madam', slipping a little white jacket over her wet bathing suit, settled down beside us. We soon learnt that, along with her extrovert manner, Mrs Sevestianov was also a very warm-hearted little lady when, being concerned that the heat might prove to be too much for me, she made a little turban out of the paper napkins and placed it on my head.

In a little while the fish soup, or *ukha* as it is called in Russia, was ready and served. We all settled down around our makeshift table to enjoy it. At this point I have to say that throughout my long life, having tasted many kinds of soups in various countries I had never any soup as good as the *ukha* prepared in a drum on the banks of the Dvina. In fact the whole of the picnic, which I know had been specially arranged for me, was one of the highlights of my visit – never to be forgotten.

All joyful events come to a close. Everything was cleared and packed away and the place left as tidy as we had found it and after the same hazardous climb aboard we set off on the return journey to Archangel. En route was a brief stop beside the lovely sandy beach where Leonid Alexeiyevich and his wife disembarked, presumably to pick up their car and drive home. I thanked Leonid for all that he had done for us. Leonid was rather shy and a man of few words but his little wife made up for it and throwing her arms around me kissed me several times. The last sight we had of this kind couple was of them standing on the path leading up to the top of the cliff and waving their hands in goodbye.

We continued our journey. The river was beautiful – a shimmering rosy haze lay over the water – but with the sun still gliding on a cloudless sky, the heat was almost unbearable. In the end, being unable to suffer it any more, I was put inside the wheelhouse.

It was a great relief to disembark in Archangel where we all went our separate ways. On the Sunday following the picnic, Misha drove us to a place called Malikh Karelakh situated some eighteen miles from Archangel. It turned out to be a museum of old Russian wooden architecture brought from other settlements in the north. The museum, which opened in 1972, is a source of great interest not only to visitors from abroad and other parts of Russia, but to the locals as well.

We left in the early morning and on our way passed many villages including one named Uima which was of special interest to me. In the previous century it was the Post House where my grandmother arrived after her interview with the Tsar in January 1881, just prior to his assassination in March by a group of revolutionaries. Uima is now a beautiful village with rows of cottages painted in different colours and flowers on the window-sills. Across the road are gardens where are grown vegetables, potatoes and fruit bushes. We have been told that in these dachas they have electricity laid on with televisions and fridges but no running water.

As we continued on our way we were surprised to see on our left a large field where there were masses of people selling or buying a great variety of goods from tights to motor cars. It transpired that this was a legalised 'black market' which was held every Sunday and where sailors were permitted to sell any articles they had brought back from abroad.

On arriving at Malikh Karelakh and leaving the car, we were met by the lovely sound of church bells ringing out a welcome, something I had not heard for many a long year. In front of us was a beautiful wooden church brought from a village in the Onega district. Here was the bell tower, the flour mill, barns, *isbas*, wash-houses and bridges – all created from wood and transported from other districts in the north. Especially lovely was a small, seventeenth-century chapel which had been relocated from another village and now stood surrounded by pines. In one of the wooden houses was a museum exhibiting articles used in the distant past. There I remember seeing an ancient sledge, a colourful *sarafan* used by the mistress of the house, the *kaftan* of her husband and many other things which memory cannot recall.

During our visit we met a newly-wed couple coming out of the church accompanied by all the guests. The bride, a pretty girl, was dressed in white and wore a long veil. They were all very friendly when we approached to wish them good fortune and exchange a few words.

The bells continued ringing out every half hour. It is a lovely part of the country surrounded by deep woods, with a feeling of peace and something of old Russia pervading the atmosphere.

We would have liked to stay on a little longer but having accepted an invitation to a tea party taking place in the afternoon had to return to Archangel.

* * * *

After lunch and a short rest we duly set off for the tea party being held in a flat occupied by a Mrs Xenia Petrovna Gemp who also bore the accolade of 'The Pride of the North'. Then in her ninety-sixth year, she was indeed a remarkable lady. An honoured member of the Geographical Society, she had led not less than thirty scientific expeditions around the White, Baltic and Kara Seas. She was also the author of several books describing various aspects of the Arctic regions. Her whole life, in fact, had been devoted to studying the history, customs and traditions of the North of Russia. She was blessed with a remarkable memory and still recalled when, as a young girl, she witnessed the great explorer Sedov, setting off from Archangel on his expedition to the North Pole. Yet like so many Russians, Xenia Petrovna did not escape her share of sorrow and had never got over the loss of her mother, who, along with four other women, was arrested and sent to the infamous labour camp in Solovky, where, starved and labouring in terrible conditions, all bar one died.

On arriving at the flat, we found the room crowded with Mrs Gemp's numerous friends. Ian Taylor also arrived with his camera crew, all set to take a film of the visit.

Mrs Gemp was sitting at the table on which was a rich display of home baking – cakes, cookies etc. She welcomed me warmly and asked me to sit beside her where she proceeded to display an old map of Archangel, which she had earlier tried to send to me, only to have it returned with the short comment that no maps are ever allowed to be sent abroad.

While we were thus engaged I was surprised by the arrival of Captain Novgorodski who had approached us on the day of the picnic and expressed his wish to give me the picture of the ice-breaker *Canada*. Determined that I should have it, he then handed it to me and after my thanks and a short conversation settled down beside Ronald. At this point Ian Taylor asked me to stand up and display the picture, but as I rose to do so, the captain, who had been talking to Ronald, suddenly collapsed and became unconscious as a result of what we assumed was a heart attack. Ian and his crew immediately left the scene and in a matter of minutes two doctors and hospital orderlies arrived with a stretcher. After a cardiograph reading the captain was taken to hospital. This incident cast a certain gloom on the guests, but with the hope that the captain would recover the party carried on. Mrs Gemp, completely calm and unperturbed, continued talking, telling me that she had known and respected my step-grandfather and babushka. She also remembered meeting my mother at some party and thinking how pretty this Scottish lady was.

We left in the early evening and on our way home Ronald told me, much to my consternation, that having caught a glimpse of the cardiogram, he knew that the captain had died prior to being taken to hospital.

His gift of the coloured print of the ice-breaker *Canada* now hangs in our dining-room.

* * * *

We had now spent two weeks in Archangel; only four days were left prior to leaving for Leningrad and then on to London and Edinburgh.

During our stay we had become acquainted with many people from various walks of life, there had been happy gatherings, parties, articles in the papers describing my arrival, interviews for the radio – yet at no time did I meet any of the friends of my youth or even a single classmate. Once, after a live interview, as we left the station the telephonist ran after us to tell me that some-one related to Valya Lazareva had called but by the time I reached the 'phone she had rung off and I was unable to trace the call. Valya, a classmate in the Gymnasium, had been my best friend with whom I had corresponded until the early Thirties when all correspondence ceased. I would have loved to have heard something about her but sadly no one 'phoned again. On looking back I now understand it was unrealistic to expect to meet any of my childhood friends as the life span of people in Russia after all their suffering and privations is much lower than that in the U.K.

Meanwhile the visits and the parties accompanied by songs and lively conversations continued. There was no feeling of restraint under *glasnost*, but once when I mentioned how much I would have liked to travel for two nights by train from St Petersburg to Archangel as I used to during my childhood, I was informed by Tanya that no foreigner was allowed to travel by train to Archangel – a statement which reminded me that the Iron Curtain was still fluttering in the background! What was it, I wondered, that the passenger could see from the window of his carriage – but I did not press for further enlightenment and perhaps Tanya herself would not have known the answer.

Apart from all the parties and outings we were well looked after by Svetlana and Misha in their house. Misha was always ready to oblige us with his car and Svetlana with Tanya's help prepared the food. Each morning we had breakfast in the kitchen – usually buckwheat porridge, tea and freshly-made pancakes and fruit when available. I was always intrigued by the method of washing the dishes. All water, hot and cold, is supplied direct from the town with no limit in each case. No basin was used nor any detergents. The hot water was turned on and allowed to flow freely over each dish, cup or saucer. The tap was not turned off until all the articles were cleaned and gleaming. They were then placed on a rack to dry, a very hygienic but rather extravagant method. It was, as one might say, coming off a broad back but the crunch came in the summer when, for a whole week, the hot water was cut off while the supply system was overhauled. Many of the citizens were prepared for this eventuality by utilising electric kettles and a water heater. Svetlana, a meticulous housewife, was constantly changing our sheets, towels, etc and washing them in the washing machine kept in the bathroom and later hanging everything out to dry in the balcony.

'What kind of people are they now in Archangel?' I was asked by my friends on our return to Scotland.

'The same as I had known in the days of my childhood,' I told them, 'just as kind, big-hearted and hospitable.'

It is an opinion also shared by many people who have travelled to Russia. The Russians are also highly intelligent people to whom education is of paramount importance and in which proficiency in foreign languages plays a big part. It never failed to amaze me how perfectly some of them spoke in English without ever having set foot in Britain. It was always a delight for me to hear Tanya exclaim in the refined tones of an English lady – 'Oh my Goodness Gracious!' Tanya is the head of the Foreign Literature Department in the Dobroluvbova District Library, Valya Golisheva is Professor of English in the University of Archangel and Olga Balaganova teaches English in what was at one time my old school but is now under another name. Many people in similar positions in Britain can travel abroad, run a car and own their house, but seventy years of repression destroyed such freedom for the average Russian. It is my belief that had the Democratic revolution of March 1917 succeeded with the Tsar holding a similar position to that of our Royal family, then Russia today would be a highly successful, prosperous and orderly country firmly established among the leading powers. She can still occupy that position if she can succeed in abolishing the mafia and stamping out corruption.

Many songs and poems have been written about the beauty and pleasures of a 'White Winter'. In reality it wasn't always so. Tanya, who at that time shared with her son a single room in an old house, found the winters very difficult to bear at times.

'When it's cold and dreary,' she recounts, 'we girls like to get together and go to the Banya, and there in the lovely warmth we undress in the washing room and scrub and beat each other with birch twigs and then later, clean and refreshed, we go to the library, drink tea and watch the video.'

*　　*　　*　　*

During the last few days of our stay in Archangel we received an invitation from Katya Menshikova to visit her mother in Solombala with whom she and her little son Maximka were staying. Katya, a talented young woman, had been a member of a student ensemble called 'Severko' – meaning a playful wind blowing in from the White Sea – who, three years earlier, in a revue at the Edinburgh Festival, had presented, with tremendous success, a wonderful exhibition of singing and dancing. I remember attending this lovely performance with Ronald and the family and later meeting the young actors outside the stage door, where, on discovering that I was also from Archangel, they had thrown their arms around me – kissing and hugging! I should have liked to have entertained them privately but even with Mr Gorbachev's *glasnost* this was not permitted. Little did I dream that the day would come when I would meet one of the performers in Archangel!

As I new very little about Solombala, Katya decided to escort us. And so, along with Tanya, we set off on what turned out to be a much longer walk than we had expected, in parts on wooden pavements raised over marshy ground – not a pleasant experience if you happened to slip off!

On reaching the house we were met with the traditional welcome of bread and salt. Inside, as usual, the table was spread with a rich variety of food accompanied with cranberry cordial and vodka. Katya's mother, who warmly welcomed us, turned out to be a remarkable lady, a member of a Russian choir who had travelled to America, France and other parts of Europe where they were enthusiastically received. Present in the party were several relatives and friends including Valya Golisheva and her daughter Natasha. We were duly introduced to everybody including a lady who was also a member of the choir and had travelled abroad. We spent a wonderful time listening to the beautiful singing of our hostess and her friend and later joined in with all the others singing in English and Russian. In the late evening Misha called for us for which we were duly grateful as I had been bothered with a very sore foot. On our way home Misha decided to show us the west bank of Solombala, which I had never seen before. It is a very beautiful part of the island overlooking a great expanse of the river. Although then past ten o'clock it was still clear daylight with the sun slowly gliding along the horizon. It was all very peaceful and strangely silent with people strolling quietly up and down the river bank and children playing nearby.

The following evening – our last Wednesday – we were invited along with Tanya to join Alexei and Shura for a farewell dinner.

We set off by bus from Solombala and duly arrived at Alexei's flat. Also present were Alesha with his wife and a very attractive teenage daughter who, when shaking hands with me, gave a quick curtsey – something I had not seen for years – which reminded me of my own childhood when young girls were always taught to curtsey when meeting elderly ladies.

We spent a pleasant evening going over old albums that Alexei produced and the pictures that I brought to show them. Alexei is a modest man and I had no idea, until I saw the photographs of him in full uniform, that he was actually a very high-ranking officer in the Russian Air Force. We had an interesting time exchanging reminiscences and, with me being so much older, relating many incidents that took place in the distant past about which Alexei had never heard previously. We likewise were interested to hear about their various exploits during the war and the times they spent later in the south where was a great abundance of fruit, vegetables and other necessities and life in general was much better than in Archangel. Shura, born in warmer climes, still regretted the transfer to the North, but to Alexei it was a case of returning home.

After a lovely dinner and the evening drawing to a close, we were presented with gifts, the nature of which I have sadly forgotten, perhaps due to being quite overwhelmed by Alesha's gift of the horns of an elk he had shot when hunting in the woods. While duly expressing our gratitude for such an unusual present I wondered vaguely how we could possibly get it home! We were eventually successful in doing so and as I write these words the antlers are gracing our hall.

At the end of the evening, having said our goodbyes, we travelled back in great comfort in the Volga – courtesy of Yuri Barashkov.

In the afternoon of the next day Misha once again drove the three of us, this time to Yuri Barashkov's flat where he had arranged to interview me for Archangel Television. On arrival we were met by the camera crew and the producer – a pleasant young woman known to be very artistic. Yuri, however, was not at home and as it was raining we gathered inside on the landing outside his flat. As we stood talking together the door on the opposite side opened and a little old lady appeared on the scene. 'Please,' she said, approaching Ron and I, 'would you care to come in?' We accepted her invitation and as we entered, a little dog barking a welcome came rushing to meet us. Inside we were a bit surprised to discover that the furnishings of the room consisted of only three chairs, a table, a cupboard with cups and saucers on top, a small cooker and nothing else. Sitting at the table was a frail old man who rose and politely shook hands with us. 'Please stay!' said his wife. 'I shall make a cup of tea.' We sat down but explained that there was no time for tea. 'I shall be very quick,' she pleaded, but with that there was a knock on the door – Yuri had arrived. I could read the disappointment in their eyes as we left – feeling humbled by such kindness in the face of dire poverty.

The interview with Yuri was all about the events described in my book. Some four months later, by now back in Scotland, I received the video tape and to my surprise discovered it included several beautiful wintry scenes with an attractive little girl, warmly clad and pulling a sledge over the snow along the avenue of birches beside the river, a very artistic presentation which in spite of being in Russian delighted all my friends.

Meanwhile, after the end of the interview we travelled back to Solombala along the river front where we were surprised to find several naval ships at anchor in the river, decorated with flags and surrounded by little boats of every description. It transpired that all this was in preparation for a Naval Review to take place on Saturday which unfortunately was the day of our departure.

*   *   *   *

In the early afternoon on Friday, Tanya Urchenko arrived to assist Tanya and Svetlana in the preparations for the final party. Meanwhile Ron and I occupied ourselves with the packing. After a prolonged struggle arranging the precious books and other presents that had been given to us around the elk horns and our belongings, we succeeded in closing the cases and were now all set to leave the following morning.

In the evening the first to arrive was Yuri with his wife Tanya followed by all our other friends. It was the final happy gathering accompanied by songs, discussions, a short speech by Yuri and finally rising and holding hands to sing *Auld Lang Syne*. Early next morning Ron and I travelled in the Volga, kindly lent by Yuri with Tanya and Misha following with all our luggage.

I still remember when crossing the bridge having a final glance at the river – silver bright in the morning sun and sadly realising that I would probably never see it again.

At the airport cousin Alexei, resplendent in his uniform, was waiting. Also present were our friends, Valya, Katya, and 'happy' Tanya with her doctor husband, Yuri and others. Tanya Klushina, who had been with us everywhere we went from the day of our arrival, was looking very sad and I myself had the unhappy feeling that I was once again saying goodbye to Archangel.

The flight was comfortable and uneventful. On arrival in St Petersburg we were met by Seryozha and Elena who informed us that their mother was expecting us for lunch. We had some difficulty in getting a taxi but showing the magic dollar did the trick. We duly arrived to a warm welcome from Elena and Natasha who had especially returned from the country to prepare the usual lavish lunch of soup, *perozhkis*, meat rolls in cabbage, cold chicken etc, accompanied by vodka and champagne. The family were eager to hear about our experiences in Archangel and we duly obliged.

We left accompanied by Seryozha and Elena in good time to catch the 'plane to London and were very grateful to Seryozha who succeeded in gaining permission to carry our luggage right up to the security gates.

In London we were met by our friends, Ken and Elizabeth McCaw, who took us to their lovely home in Harpenden. There we spent two restful days and were shown around St Albans' places of great interest such as the magnificent cathedral which we had never seen before.

On our last morning our kindly hosts drove us back to the airport where we boarded the 'plane for Edinburgh.

It was good to be back in Scotland, see the familiar places, sleep in our own beds and meet friends and relations eager to hear the details of the trip.

We settled down to our old way of life with Archangel gradually receding like a distant dream.

The autumns in Scotland are often very pleasant especially at dusk and on one such evening I decided to go for a walk on my own. Nearby was a long row of solid houses with little gardens in full bloom. I saw two men talking together across the hedge. They smiled and waved their hands. Further along was an elderly lady stripping the dead heads of her roses. She stopped to have a few words with me. As I continued on my way passing these lovely gardens and friendly people it suddenly occurred to me – what a good thing it was that my father decided to marry a Scottish bride!

Chapter 6

ONLY THE DVINA REMAINS

IN THE EARLY spring of 1992, I, along with Ronald and Michael, received an invitation from the local government to come to Archangel and join in the festivities for what is known as 'The Day of Arhangelsk' taking place on 20 June. As on the previous visit all expenses would be paid for while in Russia.

We duly arrived and on this occasion were put up in the hotel 'Pur Navolok' overlooking the river and reputed to be the best hotel in Archangel and where indeed the accommodation, food, etc. was *par excellence*.

There on our arrival, a luncheon party took place. There we met all our old friends and also discovered other relations named Gernet. Lucy Gernet is the granddaughter of my grandmother's wild brother Dmitri whom I described in my book in by no means flattering terms with which, to my relief, Lucy agreed. We had several happy meetings in her house where we also met her son Sergei and lovely daughter Tanya.

It was good to meet Alexei again, Shura, little Marina and all the other members of the family.

There were again joyful parties with all our friends but this time I found people talked openly about events that were never mentioned previously and there was also something lighthearted in the atmosphere best expressed by Lucy Gernet's remark: 'How lovely it is to go to bed and know that there will not be that terrible knock on the door.'

Sadly, in other respects the trip was a disaster. The weather unexpectedly turned bitterly cold with a penetrating wind blowing from the Arctic. No one in living memory could recall such a dreadful summer and not being prepared for it we went about in borrowed clothing. I, in a quilted coat belonging to a friend, Ronald and Michael looking like Russian Air Force officers in flying jackets lent by a friend who was an ex-pilot in the Russian Air Force.

Yet it takes more than mere cold weather to stop the natives of Archangel from making the most of their festival. Girls in their *sarafans* and young men in embroidered shirts formed circles, singing and dancing. Crowds of people were strolling up and down: men with their children on their shoulders – all eating ice-cream cones – everybody happy and cheerful, but for us too cold to stand and watch!

Unfortunately, while visiting the cemetery a few days later accompanied by Ronald and Sergei Gernet, we were caught in a heavy downpour and having to walk through knee-deep grass to reach the taxi were completely drenched, as a result of which I developed a very bad cold and became seriously ill and was confined to bed. My friend Valya, brought her friend Dr Zinaida Koshkina, who, after diagnosing that my left lung was affected, barely left my side for the whole of the following week. It was only due to her loving care that I recovered sufficiently to be able to travel back to Scotland.

Meanwhile Michael was enjoying the unique experience of being taken by 'plane to Solovki. The Solovetski Monastery at one time was a beautiful and peaceful place which I remember visiting with my parents when I was very young. Later under the rule of communism it was known as one of the most terrible gulags where thousands of helpless prisoners were tortured and starved to death while labouring in freezing conditions on the White Sea Canal. Now the monastery is gradually being reconstructed and people are once again visiting this sacred place. Michael was warmly welcomed and spent the day being shown around by the very friendly man in charge of all the work, something Michael much appreciated and has never forgotten.

On the morning following his return from Solovki, Michael flew back to Scotland. By now we also, after my recovery, were left with only four days of our stay. During this time I received an invitation from the doctor in charge of the hospital situated where once stood our house, to visit the place.

Accompanied by Ronald, Tanya and Yuri Barashkov we duly arrived there. The gates were wide open and as I walked through I was overcome by a strange uncanny feeling as if I was once again coming home from school. The kindly doctor welcomed us but as we strolled around I did not see a single trace of anything that might have reminded me of the beautiful garden created by my talented grandmother. It was actually amazing how thorough was the destruction in such a short space of time. There was no trace of the pond, nor even of the little hill on top of which stood the unique summer house – like something out of a fairy tale. I remembered it was there, on the day of our departure, that I had climbed to the turret from where could be seen the town and the river and said goodbye to them.

Gone also were the tall blue pines brought from Siberia and the beautiful poplar covered each spring with crimson pendulous catkins, a source of great delight to my brother and I who liked to gather and throw them at each other! As we continued walking I had hoped to find perhaps one of the little pebbles that used to be spread on the paths, but no – even they were gone. There were tarmac paths bordered by knee-deep grassy patches, a few young trees, bushes, a bench to rest on, a building to the left and the hospital on our right with little children waving from the top windows.

The doctor was a very friendly man and prior to our leaving presented me with the plans, showing the houses, including our own which were doomed to be destroyed when the hospital was built.

On the day prior to our departure a farewell luncheon was held in the hotel. All our friends, including the members of the Gernet family, had gathered together. Yuri Barashkov gave a short speech and early on the next day we were aboard the 'plane en route to St Petersburg where we were met by my nephew Seryzoha and Elena who once again saw us safely on to the plane for London and thence to Edinburgh.

I have since been asked at times by friends: 'How did you like your Archangel?' 'My Archangel,' I tell them, 'with the lovely old houses, gardens and churches, has long since vanished and has been replaced by rows of high-rise flats – not so pleasing to the eye, but very necessary for such a large population. What remains the same is the Dvina – lovely in the winter, sleeping under her white blanket and beautiful in the summer, lit up by the rosy glow of the setting sun while flowing serenely on her way to the sea.'